Unconditional

Unconditional

Learning to Love Your Authentic Self

Annalisa Smithson, LPC

Illustrations by Cory Derer

Illustrated by Cory Derer
Cover design by Maggie McDevitt
Edited by Pete McConnell and Marisa Solis

Published by
Animal-Assisted Therapy, LLC
152 East High Street, Suite 440A
Pottstown, PA 19464, USA

ISBN: 979-8-9859977-2-9

SUBJECT: Self-Help / Psychology

This book is dedicated to my family:
John, the love of my life,
River, our beloved kiddo, and
Benji, the dog of our dreams.

CONTENTS

CONTENTS

CONFIDENTIALITY STATEMENT

The privacy and confidentiality of my clients is of the utmost importance and held to the highest standards. None of the stories told in this book are depictions of real clients. All figures are fictional composites that represent the most typical response to a therapeutic intervention.

Introduction

You are a hardworking, well-educated, savvy individual. You give your boss your all, fill your wallet with side-gigs, and somehow make time for your nephew's popcorn fundraiser. You're kinda the shit. You're open-minded, kind-hearted, and a bona fide dog-person. Or maybe you prefer cats. Either way, you give money to the local animal shelter and try to make time to volunteer. You do these things because you're a good person.

But you struggle to balance it all: your job(s), your family, your sanity, your less-than-perfect body. You have a lot on your plate precisely because you're an engaged member of your community. And yet, no matter how many accomplishments you achieve or compliments you receive, there's this nagging voice in the back of your head pushing you around. That voice leaves you full of self-doubt. It leaves you stressed out, overwhelmed, and maybe a little lonely. It leaves you craving self-love.

Sound familiar?

Believe it or not, this is *normal*—or perhaps *common* is a better word. Americans are among the most stressed-out people in the world,[1] and for many of us, this problem goes beyond stress and reaches into the territory of mental anguish. Millions of people suffer unnecessarily from poor mental health: 17.3 million of us experience episodes of depression,[2] and nearly 40 million have experienced anxiety.[3] If you're one of these people, you know that mental health impacts every aspect of our daily lives: how we eat, sleep, move, work, and interact with the people we love. Most importantly, it affects how we feel about ourselves.

Wherever your mental health rests along the wellness spectrum, you're reading this book because you want to reduce stress. The secret to reducing stress and living a happy, satisfied life is this: unconditional self-love.

What Is Unconditional Self-Love?

What is self-love? What makes it unconditional? How do you practice it? We'll get to all those answers and more throughout this book, but first I want to help you connect with the feeling of unconditional love.

Who better to help you understand unconditional love than your faithful dog?[4] If you have a family dog, I'm betting you take really good care of him—perhaps more than your fair share. I'm also thinking that you don't mind much because you adore the little mutt. He listens without fail, wags his tail in thanks at dinnertime, greets you with kisses even when you were just getting the mail. The dog never judges you. He certainly never judges like you judge yourself. He loves you unconditionally. So your dog knows that you *deserve* unconditional love. I wonder if you know, too?

To be loved without conditions, limitations, or expectations sounds blissful. To offer such affection and appreciation to others sounds difficult, but not impossible. How does it feel to imagine loving yourself in the same way? Without judgment. Without fear. Without conditions.

You deserve to love yourself as unfailingly and as wholesomely as Doggo loves you. You could learn a lot from that pup.

Here comes the good news. You *can* love yourself unconditionally. You can treat yourself every bit as lovingly as Doggo treats you. It just requires a little rewiring of your brain.

Okay, maybe a lot of rewiring. Years, or even decades, of negative thought patterns, harsh self-talk, and heaps of self-blame will take some work to undo. But you *can* undo it.

As an animal-assisted therapy team, Benji and I work with many clients who fit this model: people who have a Ph.D. in caring for others, but barely pass the entrance exam to Self-Care 101. People like you, perhaps. There was a time when I fit that model, too.

Change Is Hard

During my counseling program at Lehigh University, I took a highly motivating and extremely frustrating class in addictions. The professor was young, intelligent, and gorgeous. He competed—and won—Spartan races. He ate a strict, nutritious, supposedly delicious "food is fuel" diet. His jokes were a little rough, but once I realized he meant well, I found him hilarious.

He walked into the classroom on day one and announced,

"If you're going to be 'healing professionals,' [air quotes] you better do more than talk the talk. You better be walkin' the walk." He strutted to the front of the classroom, muscles rippling.

"Telling your clients to quit using drugs and get a job isn't how we do therapy." (What therapist would take *that* disastrous approach?)

"Living your own healthy life is the first step to being a great therapist." Okay, he was starting to win me over.

"I challenge you," he continued, "to six weeks of healthy living. Fair warning: You're going to fail this challenge." Definitely not won over yet.

He was right, though. Painfully, embarrassingly right. Day after day we groused in our journal assignments about how hard it was to eat well, sleep eight hours, meditate daily, and work out like a Spartan. Week after week he laughingly, knowingly encouraged us to put down the Skittles and "just keep trying."

By the end of the semester, I was full of facts about how opiates affect the brain, why naloxone reverses overdose, and what treatments work well for substance use disorders. But the real lesson of Professor Spartan was this: change is hard.

Read that again: *change is hard.*

Change can be overwhelmingly, frustratingly hard.

And if a change as obviously beneficial as eating fewer Skittles is this tough, how much more debilitating must it feel to give up dope, a substance that becomes enmeshed in the brain's functioning after only one or two uses?

We'll come back to Professor Spartan's lesson later.

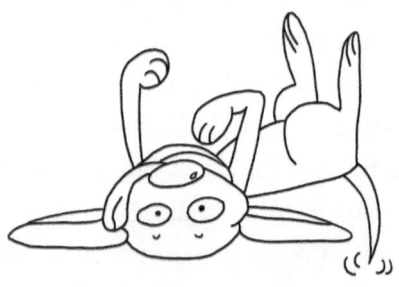

Meet Benji

Several years after meeting Professor Spartan, I met Benji. When he's in trouble, I offer up his full name, Benjamin Sisko Franklin, but usually he's a good boy who just goes by Benji. He was barely nine months old when we met, and you could tell. His puppiness shone through his black and tan coat and heart-wrenching hound dog eyes.

Benji was a rescue from West Virginia. He cowered when we said "No" too forcefully, and he was terrified of stairs. He had hookworms and a viral infection. It's easy to imagine the worst for his backstory.

I was a bit of a rescue, too, by that time. (I mean, I didn't have worms or anything.) At my lowest, I was a broke, thirty-something college student, a divorcee, and mommy to a sassy toddler. I subsisted on pizza and salad, woke up at 5 a.m. to study, and spent my weekends doing temp jobs. I also worked full-time and functioned only through the good grace of coffee. I gained thirty pounds in three years and took twice as long to finish my master's degree. My once-daily meditation practice was replaced by a minute-to-minute worry habit. In the time between graduation and adopting Benji, my circumstances had changed, but my habits and attitude felt hardwired. There was a lot to love about me, but I saw very little of it. I *felt* very little of it. It's like I wore a special pair of glasses that only showed my darkest side; but Benji saw me through rose-colored glasses—or rather, the lightest shade of grey. (Is it true that dogs don't see much color?) My point is, that like most dogs, he showed me unconditional love.

Once Benji got the all-clear from our veterinarian and trainer, he started coming to the clinic each day. His presence encouraged me to start taking daily walks and showing my pale face to the sun. The more freckles I got, the better I felt. Benji's presence in the therapy practice benefited my clients, too. He helped us build trust, communicate differently, and break down some of the barriers that exist in traditional talk therapy. He demonstrated self-love (in that way all puppies do) as well as unconditional love for the humans in the room. He created a sense of companionship as well as joyfulness that made therapy... fun.

What We Can Learn from AAT

Benji's expensive, high-quality food reminded me of Professor Spartan's "food is fuel" mantra and I started thinking about how my life had changed in the years since my Addictions class, and since Benji became my companion and co-therapist.

And then a lightbulb went on.

Change itself isn't hard.

"But wait," you're thinking to yourself, "you just said change is overwhelmingly hard and made me read it twice?!"

I was wrong. Change itself isn't hard.

Quick, compassionless change—that's what's hard.

Forcing a change that we don't believe in, don't think we deserve, don't truly want. Change that doesn't fit our values. That's what's hard. Apologies, Professor Spartan, but I respectfully disagree with your first lesson.

Gentle, empathetic change is not only possible, it's pleasurable.

If I could only show myself the acceptance, the loving-kindness, and the gentleness that Benji shows, I could achieve change relatively painlessly. I could fuel my body with nourishing food, calm my worries with the ease of meditation, sleep *all night long*, and challenge my savage self-talk. I could give up alcohol and other habits that cause more harm than good. I could learn to play again!

I revisited another of Professor Spartan's messages. "Living your own healthy life is the first step to being a great therapist." *That* I still wholeheartedly agreed with.

I was a good therapist. But I wanted to be a great therapist. I was a functioning human. But I wanted to be a healthy, happy, fully authentic human. With Benji's help, I've achieved both. Benji and I would like to help you achieve your version of a healthy, happy human. We want you to love your authentic self the same way Doggo loves you: unconditionally.

All it takes is rewiring your brain.

Yep, that's all.

I'm going to teach you a variety of self-help techniques that are rooted in cognitive behavioral therapy (CBT), narrative therapy, and of course animal-assisted therapy. These are skills that will empower you to fully care for your heart, mind, and body. You'll learn to challenge, alter, and eliminate thoughts like:

"I suck."

"I'm never going to get it."

"I'm an awful parent."

"I should be a better worker."

"I'm 'fat' and full of cheese."

And on and on in the "I'm the problem" loop.

I'm going to teach you to don Doggo's rose-colored glasses when you look in the mirror. You deserve that.

When Pavlov's puppy[5] began drooling each time he heard the bell ring, it was because his puppy brain was rewired to associate bells with treats. We can do that too. Animal-assisted therapy (AAT) is full of powerful lessons we can learn from animals and nature. But there's more to it than just metaphors and models. In AAT, we lean on the authenticity of the dog or other pet to be present and mindful during therapy. We use those skills to notice what our human brains are telling us, and to refocus on what matters. We lean on the animal's need for fresh air, sunshine, and clean water to give ourselves the same. We commit to self-care by caring for the animal. In a way, the animals are leading *us* by example. You'll learn more about AAT throughout this journey, and in doing so, you'll learn more about yourself.

How to Use This Book

What follows in this book is not only an exploration of the problems we often face when practicing self-love, but also some solutions to those problems. There are twenty-one chapters in this book, and each one offers an Act of Unconditional Self-Love for you to practice. These are short, snack-size chapters that can easily be devoured before breakfast. You could conceivably read one chapter per day, practice the prescribed act of self-love, and by the time you reach the end—in twenty-one days—you will have created a foundation of unconditional self-love.

Can you really form a new habit in 21 days? The answer, as in most of psychology, is an unsatisfying *maybe*. Dr. Maxwell Maltz, author of Psycho-Cybernetics and the first to notice this 21-day pattern, would say yes, absolutely! Dr. Phillipa Layla and her research team at University College London suggest it actually takes around 66 days for the human brain to catch on to a new habit. I've seen clients create lasting change after only 3 sessions! Each of us is starting from a different place in our wellness journey *and that's okay*. Your best friend may devour this book in 21 days while you stretch it out to 66 and your mom calls you in a year thanking you for the recommendation. Each of your unique experiences is valid. Honor your boundaries and offer yourself compassion and patience as you develop your own timeline for this journey.

Each chapter includes a section titled "Today's Act of Unconditional Self-Love." The daily act is an invitation for you to do one thing that boldly, unequivocally expresses love for yourself. You will be asked to create a love-list, craft a vision-board, and learn the loving-kindness meditation, for example. Maybe the thought of doing so feels silly or indulgent or bizarre. But you won't know till you try, and self-love won't become a habit unless you do it—so please don't skip these activities. They're designed to make a difference.

Each chapter ends with several journaling prompts designed to help you rewrite your story. These prompts are meant to draw the problem of self-criticism out of you and give you space to observe it. Your journal is a powerful tool for self-exploration and healing and will become the foundation of your "wellness toolbox." Plan to write in your journal (paper or digital) daily. You can take as much time as you need for your reflections, but as little as 15 minutes should do the trick. Please do not skip this work. Make journaling a part of your commitment to practicing self-love.

In order to make your new attitude of self-love a life-long endeavor you'll need to intentionally turn this into a habit. Try pairing the journaling with a habit you've already formed. Social psychologists teach us that new habits are created when we associate the desired behavior with a cue and a reward.[6] For example, if you're in the habit of enjoying a hot cup of coffee each morning, plan to do your writing while the coffee is brewing and hold off that delicious first sip until you've completed the journaling prompt.

Ready, Set, Love

I'm honored to be your guide on this journey to self-love. I know from personal experience and from my clients that practicing self-love might feel selfish or pointless at first. But I'm here to tell you that those are your negative thoughts talking, and you're soon going to learn to tell them to hush. Remember, too, that self-love is profoundly important to your whole-body health. Freeing yourself from stress, overwhelm, depression, anxiety, and any other feeling that keeps you from living your best life—begins with loving yourself. Unconditionally.

So get ready to earmark the next 21 days on your calendar. And grab a pet too; dog or not, a furry friend can be a terrific passenger on your journey. Your road trip to a rewarding life starts now.

Day 1: Understand That You're Not the Problem

We've already mentioned the stress, guilt, loneliness, and utter lack of time to accomplish it all. But believe it or not, that's not the problem. The problem is that we think *we're* the problem. We spend a lifetime receiving messages that tell us to be more, do more, and spend more. Be a better parent/partner/person. Do more multitasking/shopping/planning. Spend more time/money/energy on anything and everything except the real you. What kind of pressure do you experience? What are you constantly asked to do more of? Pinterest virtuosos would have us believe that if, by some strange, unpredictable reason (like humanness), we somehow inexplicably fail at becoming a Super, it's definitely because we suck. (Go ahead and dip something in that steaming pot of sarcasm-cheese. You deserve a fondue break.)

So how, exactly, did I become the problem?

Okay, to be clear, you're not the problem. The problem is that *you think* you're the problem. Let me explain:

How Human Socialization Works

Humans are social creatures. As children, we learn about ourselves through a process of socialization. You created your original self-image by noticing what your role models were saying and doing. (Remember this for later: you couldn't know what your role models were actually thinking.) Sociologist George Herbert Mead called this process "social behaviorism." He suggested that much of our social interaction grows out of what he termed a "conversation of gestures," much like two dogs sniffing and circling one another. But we also use conscious communication, i.e. language, to enhance our interactions. In both cases, we interpret and internalize what others convey to us as the norm. Simply put, we reflect those around us.

Unfortunately (or fortunately for some), our parents are not wholly in charge of conveying societal norms. We learn about what "normal" is from our teachers, peers, coaches, movie characters, fictional heroes, commercials, neighbors, even our pets. (How many of us first learned where babies come from when Fluffy got knocked up? Just me?)

As a society we tackle a great many problems: sexism, racism, homophobia, hypermasculinity, stigma against mental illness, addiction, surviving rape, and so on. These are systemic problems, the symptoms of which sneak into our everyday lives.

One quick example before we abandon the sociology lesson and get back to you and your dog. This is how a systemic problem, in this case stigma against overweight people and perceptions of the female body, was internalized by a role model and taught to her little sister.

During one of my workshops, I asked the attendees to commit to a single self-care activity. Catherine raised her hand and said, "I'm going to be starting a Keto diet so I can take better care of my body." This ignited a lively conversation about whether diets count as self-care. It even led us through an exploration of what it's like to be called "skinny." Catherine went on to explain that she has focused on her weight ever since her pre-teens, when her older sister unhelpfully advised her to lose some weight before high school. Twenty years later, she still thinks about that advice and subconsciously believes women experience joy primarily when they're skinny. During that conversation, Catherine said, "Oh, I know I'll never be one of those bubbly, skinny girls! I just want to be healthy." She had internalized a societal norm through a series of conversations with her sister—and through other interactions with people who gave her similar messages—and grew up believing that her body was a problem. Except she didn't say, "I want my body to be skinny." She said she'll never be skinny. She considered herself the problem. If skinny equals happy in her internal norms system, then she's enduring a hell of a lot of pain just by saying that out loud. She internalized that message and carried it as a burden for twenty years.

Catherine's struggle is one that many of us can relate to. We learn that other people are happier when they fit into the square box, so we scramble to shove our round selves into that same box. When we don't fit, we blame ourselves for not being like those other people—for not fitting into their box. For not being square enough.

My personal version of this hell happened in academia. I had a bad case of imposter syndrome made worse by perfectionism. Somewhere in my youth, I internalized a message about "smart people" and believed that my happiness lay on the other side of a doctorate. If I could only achieve more—the grades, the degree, the publications—then I'd be smart, successful, and, ultimately, happy. Until then I was an imposter and an imperfect one at that, so how could I be smart, successful, or happy? The negative loop in my brain made me anxious and exhausted. Just like Catherine, I was preoccupied with a self-image that didn't fit what I believed was normal. I thought I was the problem.

Your Own Ideals? Or Society's?

We all internalize some idea of what it means to be normal. Many of us want to fit in and be square. That's just how human socialization works. When we fall short of that ideal, many of us begin thinking we have a problem. The trouble really starts when our belief that we *have* a problem morphs into the belief that we *are* the problem. Negative self-talk, nagging guilt, and oftentimes shame all grow out of that single idea. And all that negative self-talk starts chipping away at our self-love. So how do we fix this? I'm so glad you asked.

Today's Act of Unconditional Self-Love

If you have a bookshelf full of half-written journals, thank yourself for having such lovely taste in books, and select your favorite one for this journey. If not, it's time to go shopping! Look for a cover that tickles your fancy: artwork or a mantra that makes you smile. As you begin each chapter over the next 21 days, you can take a moment to enjoy the cover art of your journal. Give yourself an additional simple pleasure by buying a great pen in a color that speaks to you.

The tactile experience of writing (and crossing something off a list) can feel super satisfying, but if paper journals aren't for you, try an online journal. One benefit of digital journaling is that voice-to-text makes it easy to capture your stream of conscious thoughts. You're likely to be carrying your digital journal with you at all times, so you can pause and reflect on your 'Act of Unconditional Self-Love' at any point in the day.

Once you've chosen your paper or digital journal, open to the next blank page and respond gently to any inner criticisms that came up while you were reading this chapter. For example:

Inner critic: "Bingo! I'm 'fat' like Catherine."

You: "Neither Catherine nor I need to listen to this. My weight has nothing to do with my authentic self."

Inner critic: "What is this self-love bullshit? Who has time for this every day?"

You: "It's scary and exciting to imagine being loved unconditionally!"

Inner critic: "The dog doesn't love you unconditionally; he just wants a good meal."

You: "YOU LEAVE DOGGO OUT OF THIS."

Today's Journaling Prompts

1. What is self-love?
2. How do I show love to others?
3. How does my pet (or an animal I had in the past) show love? What can I learn from this?

Day 2: Give Yourself Some Puppy Love

So, now we know the problem is that we bought into the bull-shit. It's not our fault; we were children, after all. We hadn't yet developed a logical, reasoning prefrontal cortex in our brains when we were bombarded with messages about how to be normal. We were socialized by unwitting role models to seek a norm defined by skinny bodies and fat wallets (or perhaps it was hot sex and massive houses; or perfect grades and accolades; or something unique to you). When we fell short of the unlikely "normal" we wondered what, exactly, was wrong with us. We decided we were the problem. We created a habit of negative self-talk that damaged our most crucial asset: self-love.

The Radical Notion of Self-Love

Self-care is hard enough for people to commit to, but self-love? Self-love is a radical notion. But there are some people who come by "self-love" naturally. From the incessant and questionable licking of his lower bits, I'm going to assume Doggo has "self-love" down pat. I also think children start off with great potential for self-love. Let me tell you a quick story about that:

Soon after my daughter learned to write, she asked for a journal. She chose a fuzzy pink diary with a picture of a puppy on the front. (Awww.) It had a lock and a key. It was a kindergartner's dream. She opened it up and proudly wrote her name inside the front cover. Then she asked me how to spell "secret." She told me I'm allowed to read it "because family doesn't keep secrets," but no one else could touch the prized diary. Then she created the coolest journaling exercise. She called it "River's Love List." One by one, she named all of her classmates, family members, pets, and neighbors, asking me to spell each one. After completing three solid pages, she set down the pencil and proudly recited the names.

"River, you're missing someone really important on your Love List," I told her.

"Nuh-uh. Benji's on it." (Be still, my heart.)

"But it's River's Love List. So who else should be on it?" I pushed.

She rolled her eyes, "Just tell me, mommy." Cheeky little monkey.

"You! You should be on your own Love List! Rivlet, put yourself at the very top!"

She giggled self-consciously and squeezed her name into numero uno. Then we pretended to make a YouTube video about Love Lists. (Hey, I'm a twenty-first-century parent!)

Whether you're five years old or forty-five, you deserve to be on your own Love List. And it's a damn shame that not including your own name is pretty normal.

Inviting Self-Love to Fill the Gap

The solution to this problem isn't an easy one to implement, but it is simple to understand: We stop seeing ourselves as the problem. We stop carrying the problem and acknowledge that we picked it up in the first place. (Remember that behavioral socialization process?)

We dig the problem out of our essential selves and place it on the table in front of us. We look at it, understand it, and decide what to do with it. Put it in a box and save it for later? Hand it off to our children? Or... do we shape the problem into something new?

And in that big hole the problem left behind? That breezy, new space inside our essential self? What do we do with that? I propose we fill it with love! Fill it with self-love that rivals even Benji's unconditional adoration. Fill it with the kind of love that's given without stipulations or strings. Fill it—and ourselves—with puppy love.

You've heard the term "self-care" before. Facebook memes and "Top Ten Ways to Treat Yourself" blogs show us pictures of steamy, candlelit bubble baths. Search for "self-care ideas" and there's no end to the lists of creative ways to pamper yourself. But self-care alone isn't enough. Self-care is really just a set of tools to help you cultivate self-love.

There are many ways to stop seeing ourselves as the problem and create change in our lives. Every counselor, social worker, and psychologist has a different perspective on where problems come from and how to effect change. Narrative therapy, cognitive-behavioral therapy (CBT), and animal-assisted therapy are three possible approaches. Every client has their own theory, too. Since you're taking the journey through these pages, you probably have some belief or hope that self-help and bibliotherapy are good solutions to your problem. I agree with you. I also believe in the healing power of animals and nature. Just know that your efforts in the past were not wasted. You will heal. "Buying into the bullshit" is just one way of looking at the problem; and replacing the bullshit with puppy-love is just one way of solving that problem.

Let's return to Catherine, my workshop attendee who told herself she'd be happy if she lost some weight. She had internalized this message of "fatness" and unhappiness. She spent years telling herself she'd enjoy life more if she lost some weight. When she lost some weight, she didn't feel the promised happiness. Instead of questioning the message—i.e., the problem—she questioned her efforts and herself. She assumed that she hadn't lost enough weight to achieve that happiness yet. The negative thoughts reinforced the lesson her sister had (unconsciously) taught her so many years ago and then took on a life of their own. It became a vicious cognitive loop. I asked Catherine to consider a different self-care activity to put into action. Something unrelated to food, exercise, or weight loss. She reluctantly met me halfway. She decided to show up to all her yoga classes over the next month. Four weeks later when I followed up with her, she had experienced a breakthrough. For the first time during yoga she had achieved a meditative state.

"I've never been able to meditate," she told me. "I always got bored and fell asleep during Savasana!" She sounded so proud of herself. Her voice rang with surprise, excitement, and—dare I say—happiness. She was experiencing a simple pleasure—the best kind—and seemed unaware that this pleasure had eclipsed her sister's terrible advice. The problem (as she saw it) of her body's weight was probably still there, but she had separated herself from it. She gave herself space from it. And in the process, she managed to find a bit of long-overdue happiness. But the problem (as I saw it) of believing her body was a problem was still there. If we had been working one-on-one in a clinical setting, I would have encouraged Catherine to spend some time observing both problems now that she had created some space in herself. I would have taught her specific skills to tackle the problem if it tried to creep back into her. And I would have encouraged her to enhance the happiness she had experienced in meditation by continuing to explore her mind, body, relationships, spirit, and sexuality.

Catherine took the plunge into therapy (with another clinician) and is happier than ever. I strongly recommend the same to all my readers and workshop attendees. Self-help books and long walks with Doggo are essential parts of a self-care regime, but they aren't always enough. Counseling is a powerful tool that helps us make sense of all the messages, good and bad, that we're bombarded with. It helps us set achievable, values-driven goals. A good therapist can call the bullshit when they see it and help you separate it from the real you. So, here's my disclaimer: don't rely solely on dogs and books. Go see a therapist who can help you achieve the healing you deserve. And remember, sometimes it takes a little trial and error to find the right therapist for you.

In the meantime, practice small, simple steps to enhance your quality of life. You will slowly but surely learn to love yourself unconditionally (just like Doggo does).

Today's Act of Unconditional Self-Love

Pick one person from your Love List (see below) and ask them what they love most about you. Even if your dog is near the top of your list, I'm suggesting that you select a human, as conversation is easier. Accept what your person says without argument, without doubt, and without input from your inner critic. Take in their raw, unabridged answer and write it in your journal for posterity.

Today's Journaling Prompts

1. Who is on my Love List?
2. On a scale of 1 to 10, how much do I love myself? Why?

3. On a scale of 1 to 10, how much do I deserve to be loved? Is there something I need to do/be/have in order to deserve love?

Day 3: Embrace Change

How does change happen in your life? Do you leap into the deep end, feet first? Do you inch through the shallow end, letting yourself acclimate slowly? Does someone have to drag you into the water, kicking and screaming? Some people embrace change in their lives. Most do not.

From a CBT perspective, we say that change happens through awareness and intentionality. You learn about your own brand of negative patterns, patterns that could be enmeshed in your cognitions, emotions, or behaviors. You learn to recognize signs of your unhelpful patterns in action. Then you slowly and methodically counteract those patterns. You interject a new way of thinking, feeling, and behaving into your everyday life.

Your Brain on Change

From a neurological perspective, you're asking your prefrontal cortex to help you engage in neuroplasticity (new growth and change in your brain). You're using the logical mind to create lasting changes in the brain. Imagine that your brain is a rich, dense forest with lots of trees and underbrush. There are trails tamped into the ground where the underbrush has been pushed aside. Those existing trails are the easiest path to traverse in your brain, so you use them most often. Those trails are your patterns. You may have discovered that some of the trails aren't very safe—they take you too close to a bear's den or a cliff's edge. So now you have to do the hard work of cutting new trails and exploring new paths. This new trail is a pattern you're adopting in your life—a new way of thinking or behaving. As Robert Frost once wrote, "Two roads diverged in a wood, and I— / I took the one less traveled by, / And that has made all the difference."

Let's say you want to reduce the amount of alcohol you drink. You have a consistent habit of pouring yourself a glass of wine after dinner every night. It helps you relax, tastes nice with dessert, and is part of your daily routine. This habit is the existing trail. In order to cut a new trail, you have to recognize the negative patterns, the parts of your thinking, feeling, and behavior that don't serve you: "I need wine to relax" or "I've always done it this way, just like my parents and their nightcap." These are examples of cognitive distortions that support your old patterns. As you're blazing a new trail in the forest of your brain, you actively challenge the old thoughts and develop new ways of thinking (new cognitions) about wine, relaxation, your routine, and your parents. Those new thoughts lead to new behaviors. This is how change happens in your brain and your life. You change your inner self to change your outer self.

The Transtheoretical Model of Change

James and Janice Prochaska taught the Transtheoretical Model of Change[7] to help therapists and clients better grasp the change experience, whether it is quitting smoking, eating healthy, reducing alcohol consumption, or changing any other worrisome behavior. They posit that there are five stages of change, and it's helpful to know where you are in the cycle. These are:

1. Precontemplation
2. Contemplation
3. Preparation
4. Action
5. Maintenance

Relapse/Recycle is an additional item that isn't included as a stage, but which is an important part of the process for many people.

It helps to think of these stages like a hot summer day by the sea:

When you're in the **precontemplation** stage, you're lying on the shore sunbathing. You feel warm and comfortable and can't imagine why you'd ever want to make a change.

In the **contemplation** stage, you remember that sunbathing on a summer afternoon can sometimes get hot. You know the temperatures will rise later, and you know, intellectually, that people like you cannot remain in the sun. But you can't see yourself doing anything about it just yet. For now, you're choosing to remain in the sun with your two human feet firmly in the sand.

In the **preparation** stage, you realize that it will soon be unbearably hot, and you think about how you might deal with it. You edge over to the water and dip your toes in, just to feel it. You begin telling the important folks in your life that you will make a significant change soon.

In the **action** stage, you've accepted that it's too damn hot on dry land. You dive into the sea and start doggy paddling. You keep your head above water. You feel cooled down and relaxed. But you also feel nervous at the new experience. You worry about tiring out before you get the hang of things. You ask for help to keep swimming.

In the **maintenance** stage, you've grown fins and a mermaid tail (figuratively speaking). You dive beneath the water and swim to your heart's content at regular intervals before you allow yourself to get too hot. The change is fully integrated: it's your new lifestyle. Perhaps you start teaching other people how to transition from human to mermaid. The choice to swim has to be deliberate as well as natural because we're trying to conquer a problem or change a habit.

Relapse isn't a necessary or guaranteed stage, but it happens often enough to mention. Many people experience moments when they miss their old lifestyle. They fall back into old patterns of thinking and behaving. They head back to the shore for a quick stroll "just for old time's sake" and they get stuck there. Fortunately, it's usually just a matter of time before they remember how bad the old patterns were (how hot it gets out there) and begin contemplating the change once again. After all, whoever heard of a mermaid who never touches water?

Let's go back to the problem of too-much-wine and see how the stages of change fit. A person who ultimately decides to make a change in their life by drinking less alcohol (and remember you don't have to be an addict to want this kind of change!) might be engaging in the following self-talk during each stage:

Precontemplation: "I don't have a problem. Who doesn't enjoy some wine with their dinner? I like to relax at night and it's not like I'm an alcoholic."

Contemplation: "I wonder if other people drink wine every single night? Is it weird to be drinking wine when I'm at home alone on a Tuesday night?"

Preparation: "Hey mom, do you think I drink too much wine? I'm thinking about cutting back. What's the best way to make a change like this?"

Action: "I just researched what a healthy amount of alcohol consumption is for someone my age and I'm committing to drinking 1 glass of wine per night, no more than 3 nights per week. During my usual after-dinner drink, I'm switching to fancy tea. I'm using this app to hold me accountable."

Maintenance: "I changed my unhealthy wine habit slowly and gently over the past 6 months and I feel great. All this green tea has made my skin look great. I will keep holding myself accountable!"

Relapse: "It's the holidays, I think I deserve a few extra drinks this week. I know I said the same thing last week. And the week before. Uh-oh."

Awareness Before Action

Most people want to jump directly from contemplation to action stage. I want to encourage you to wait. You probably have a good grasp of the changes you want to make by reading this book. You're the expert on you, after all—the top dog. Trust me, though, it takes time (and contemplation and preparation) before any of us are ready to jump into action. But if you insist, here's a simple and important action step: start tracking your problem through daily journaling. If you want to quit smoking, log every cigarette you smoke. If you want to start eating vegetables, log every veggie you eat. If you want to create a more positive mindset, log every overtly negative or positive thought you notice.

Don't do anything else. Don't judge or criticize yourself. Don't beg yourself to change. Don't even try to change yet. Just track the problem. Awareness leads to improvement for most problems. One of the ways people often sabotage their good effort is by starting too quickly or tackling too many problems at once. Go slowly, method-ically, and gently. The first step is always awareness—not action.

We've covered a lot of ground from the transtheoretical model of change, to the CBT technique for initiating change, and even ex-plored the neurological components of how change happens. There is another way. Change can happen gradually and painlessly when we use the power of narrative.

The Power of Language

Humans love to hear stories. As children we learned what is "normal" and expected of us through stories. We learned to embrace our culture through stories, even as we learned to escape in the same way. Stories help us express our identity, relate to other people, and understand the world. Narrative therapists believe that stories have the power to enact change in our lives. Narrative therapists, you may recall, are the same folks who encourage us to externalize problems. They want us to make choices and take chances based on our authentic selves—separate from the problems that mistakenly define us. One of the core techniques of narrative therapy is telling your story.

Every time we tell our story we gain confidence and mastery over our lived experiences. We create distance between ourselves and our problems and learn to tell the story with a new perspective. This inevitably gives way to new storylines for the next chapter of our lives. It is especially powerful when there is a trained therapist in the room to help identify the "absent but implicit"—those parts of the story that the narrator is necessarily blind to. But it doesn't have to happen in the therapy room. Part of the reason Alcoholics Anonymous and other 12-step programs are so powerful, is because they offer fellowship. They offer a room full of people who bear witness to your story. A small group trusted friends or confidantes can also create this space for you.

As you continue to work your way through this book, I hope you will begin telling your story in a new and compassionate way. I hope you use your journal to practice talking about yourself with love and kindness. Try writing alternative endings to unhappy stories you've been telling yourself for too long. Try writing as though the narrator adores the protagonist. After all, you're both the author and the hero of your own story.

Today's Act of Unconditional Self-Love

Tell your story to someone. The story about your problem and how you're overcoming it. But commit to using powerful, positive language. Highlight your strengths and laugh through your growth areas. Imagine a unique outcome to your story and tell it in the present tense.

Today's Journaling Prompts

Tap into your inner sociologist and answer the Big Questions for yourself:

1. Why do problems develop in my life?
2. How do people create change?
3. How do I create change?

Day 4: Ask Yourself the Miracle Question

"What kind of answers do people normally give for the 'miracle question'?" My client asked nervously.

"If I told you that, I'd give away the magic!" I answered.

She half-smiled at the journal lying open in her lap, but I could sense her worry.

"Jo," I told her gently, "there are no right or wrong answers. It's your life. You get to imagine your own miracle. Your ideal."

She nodded, looking relieved for a moment, having won the latest battle with her inner perfectionist. She picked up her pen and started writing. Benji hopped off the couch and left her to her creative work. He would come back if he was needed.

What, exactly, is the "miracle question"? So glad you asked.

The miracle question is a simple but powerful therapy visualization technique co-created by Solution-Focused Brief Therapy founders, Steve de Shazer, Insoo Kim Berg, and their colleagues.[8] There are many variations of the technique, suited to children, families, adults, and couples. This technique is important to do in the therapy room, with a trained counselor. Part of the power of this exercise is in the slow, meditative quality of the asking. It gives your creative brain time to construct a full answer in your imagination. The short version of the miracle question is this: "A miracle has happened in your life—what's different now?" However, it is important to walk through the visualization step by step.

The truth is, there are no "normal" answers to the miracle question. Responses swing wildly from resurrecting the dead to realizing world peace. Some people keep it simple, imagining a quiet cup of gourmet coffee just for themselves each morning, enjoying it before the family wakes up. It may not feel like a miracle for everyone, but for a stressed-out, overworked parent who leaps out of bed, shakes the kids awake, and runs ragged for the next eighteen hours, a bit of peace and quiet can feel magical. We all have the potential for magic in our lives, but few of us know how to tap into it. The miracle question helps us envision that magic at work. It's the first step to creating our own miracle.

In my miracle world, I greet the sun as it rises each morning, welcoming the warm potential of the day. Benji is asleep at my feet, of course. I send my happy, healthy family off to start their days, and I notice that I'm genuinely excited for my day of work. I'm a successful entrepreneur. My practice is staffed by well-paid, hardworking clinicians, who also feel fulfilled in their work. Books line the walls, creating that unique paper-and-glue scent we bibliophiles love to luxuriate in. The place is surrounded by trees and walking trails— the healing power of nature at our fingertips. There are happy, healthy (well-trained) dogs playing in the greenspace. It's a place of healing for everyone who visits, clients and staff alike. It's a most unusual therapy practice, and it works.

Now I'll give away the punchline. It's not actually a miracle at all. Perhaps a windfall of start-up cash would feel like a miracle, but the brick-and-mortar is not actually the point. The feeling I get when I talk about my miracle—that's the point. Understanding what I would experience from this "miracle" is the critical part of the exercise. When I imagine my miracle world, I feel inspired, confident, and motivated. I feel surprise and a little bit of self-doubt. I feel happy. And I feel hesitant to sit with those feelings. While the answers themselves never fit a "norm," the outpouring of emotion is universal.

Envision Your Ideal Life

I've adapted the following exercise to help you visualize your ideal life. It won't pack as much punch as it would if you were addressing a problem in therapy and processing "the miracle question" with a trained counselor. Even so, there is no harm in envisioning your ideal life.

Step One

Read the following paragraph slowly. Before jumping into answer mode, read it again. You may even want to copy it into your journal, so your brain is forced to slow down to the pace of your handwriting.

"Imagine going home tonight knowing in my heart that there's a solution to my problem. I climb into bed with a 'tip of the tongue' sensation. I fall asleep comfortably and while I'm sleeping, a miracle happens. I don't wake up right away. The miracle takes care of itself while I get my rest. In the morning my body and mind awaken feeling refreshed. I sense that the miracle has happened. I notice something different. What is it I'm noticing?"

Step Two

Close your eyes and fully immerse yourself in your imagination for several minutes. Let yourself explore this miracle. Let yourself notice what is different in your environment and in your internal landscape.

Step Three

After exploring your imagination, open your eyes and continue writing in your journal. Answer each question in turn.

1. What does the room or space look like?
2. What can you hear?
3. Are there any smells or tastes in this miracle world? What is special about these foods and fragrances?
4. If people are speaking, can you identify the speakers? What are they saying?
5. Best of all, how do you feel[9] right now?

As you construct the miracle world in your mind, you may notice your confidence and motivation growing. Your self-doubt may dwindle. Ideally, the positive feelings stick with you even after you open your eyes and finish writing. The miracle question helps us envision the solutions to our problems, yes, but it can do more than that. It can give us insight into our emotional landscape. Let's go back to Jo's miracle:

"I'm waking up in a house that is mine, but it's not where I live now, ya know?" Jo's eyes are closed and there's a crease in her forehead, like she's concentrating hard. "It's bright and sunny because I was able to sleep late. It looks... homey. One of those corny 'Home Is Where the Heart Is' plaques is on the wall."

As she lapses into silence, I prompt her. "What else?"

"I'm just surprised. There's someone in bed with me. My husband."

"What can you hear?"

"His breathing. And some sounds. Outside the door there's talking. We have kids. I never wanted kids before. I'm almost forty now and I'm worried it's too late—"

She opens her eyes and brushes away tears. I wait for a few moments, giving her space. Then I invite her to come back to her miracle world. She describes the smell of clean laundry and the taste of breakfast foods. She talks about the family she has—her sisters and parents—and the family she wants—a husband and kids. When I ask her how she's feeling, she hesitates.

"I don't always know how I'm feeling. Sometimes I think I don't have feelings."

"I promise you have emotions," I tell her. "It's part of the human condition." We both glance at Benji, who stares back at us with the sad intensity of a hound dog not being petted. He jumps back onto the couch and gives her an unsolicited lick, breaking all the therapy dog rules. "Maybe emotions aren't exclusive to humans," I concede.

Jo takes a breath, revived by the short distraction Benji had offered her. "I'm feeling sad and worried and... maybe confused? Independence is really important to me and I never wanted a family. But now that I'm nearly forty years old, I've changed my mind. I was never the princess wedding girl. I don't care about that. But NOW I want a husband and kids?" She seems incredulous of herself. "What if it's too late?"

"What if it's not?" I counter with my usual directness. "What else did you feel?"

Jo smiles despite herself. "Happy. Warm, I guess." I hand her an emotions chart—a trusty stand-by in my office—and she continues. "Serene. Trusted. Valued. Loved." Her tears had started again, but they were a different kind of tears now.

The miracle question can be a powerful experience, so it helps to have someone to process it with. But you can do it in the privacy of your own journal, too. Just be gentle with yourself.

We often surprise ourselves by the image we construct in our miracle world. It's surprising because, in life, it's easy to get caught up in goals and activities that don't lead us to our miracle. Even Benji gets distracted from his miracle world by things as small as squirrels. We find ourselves focusing on jobs that aren't fulfilling, relationships that aren't healthy, and projects that don't feed our creative souls. It's also surprising how often the answer to the miracle question isn't a miracle at all. Even people who wish for impossible things like time travel or spaceships are really just yearning for a specific feeling or opportunity. Perhaps a chance to start fresh in their tired career. Or perhaps a feeling of wonder and adventure. By processing not just the answer to the miracle question, but also how it feels to envision the miracle, we can achieve deep, revealing insights into our needs.

Today's Act of Unconditional Self-Love

Ask yourself the miracle question. Slow down and write not only the prompts in your journal, but also your answer to the question. Take time to notice how you feel as you explore your answer. No one-word answers! Use the emotion chart in the Worksheets section of this book to help you articulate your feelings. Embrace your emotions as you write. Don't shy away from negative emotions, but don't neglect the positive ones either.

Today's Journaling Prompts

1. What is my miracle?
2. What would be different in my life after my miracle happens?
3. How do I feel imagining my miracle?

Day 5: Get to Know Your Emotions

In the last chapter, we talked about the miracle question, a visualization technique that can help you imagine a better life. I asked, "If a miracle happens after you go to sleep tonight, what would be different when you wake up?" Benji often works overtime following this exercise because clients tend to feel emotional. When the tears start to flow, nothing is more grounding than looking down and seeing a pup's head resting on your lap. But the tears themselves are worth noticing. The feelings are worth feeling. I often ask my clients not to take action immediately following the miracle question. Instead, I ask them to "stay with the feeling." By sitting with our emotions in these relatively safe, contained moments, our mental health and wellness improve. We set a foundation for later growth and lasting action. By staying with the feelings, we are essentially working on our "emotional landscape."

I love talking about emotions, but I didn't always love it. In fact, I remember walking into one of my clinical courses years ago coiled like a watch spring, wound tight by practicum, journaling, supervision, and personal therapy. I dropped my books on the table with a dramatic thud and announced at the top of my lungs, "I'm SO SICK of talking about my feelings!" That was one week into the course. Luckily, I was surrounded by counselors-in-training and received empathy rather than rolled eyes. At first, I thought I was barking up the wrong tree, but after the course was finished, I knew that more bark and less bite was the key. I had experienced the freedom of embracing all my feelings, "good" and "bad." I went inward to explore my emotional landscape and came out fulfilled. I even took the risk of talking about my feelings to several important people in my life, which served to strengthen those relationships. I grew to love talking about emotions.

Hollywood has created an annoying, sometimes damaging trope we think of as "The Therapist": sitting behind the couch while the client stares at the ceiling, scribbling furiously in a notebook, asking, "And how does that make you feel?" Most real therapists prefer authentic eye contact, and we tend to avoid writing while you're talking for that reason. But asking about your feelings—that's a staple of good therapy. How can you improve your emotional health if you don't talk about your emotions? If you can't even identify your emotions?

Getting Unstuck

Clients often tell me they feel "stuck," "numb," or just unable to feel. This is especially common for people who have experienced trauma and for the addicted population. Benji and I spend a lot of time helping people experience their emotions in real time. Identifying our emotions is an advanced skill in the Human Handbook; and communicating about our feelings to a loved one takes up an entire chapter. It makes sense. Who likes to talk about being sad, let alone actually feeling and facing the sadness? This even happens to folks who are typically pretty good at articulating their feelings.

I was painfully reminded of the human desire for emotional armor very recently—when I sat down to write this chapter, in fact.

My sister, who is also my best friend, came home from California for a week. It was a brilliant visit. We never laugh so much apart as we do together. We enjoyed several days in the sunshine, slugging iced coffee, cracking bad jokes, and belly laughing until our faces hurt. On Monday, it was time for her to leave. The plan was to write for two hours, wake my sister up for a last cup of coffee, and then depart separately for work and to the airport. I sat and stared at a blank page for two full hours. Type, backspace, type, backspace, type, backspace. I had a bad case of writer's block and no idea what was causing it. I felt like I was chasing my own tail. Finally, I switched off the computer and got my sister out of bed. We said our good-byes and parted ways. It wasn't until I was sitting in the car, zoning out on my morning commute, that it hit me. I was sad. I missed my sister. The tears started flowing and an annoying little voice in the back of my head pointed out that my writer's block came from the same place that my feelings blocker came from. I had cut myself off from the sadness and had effectively shut down my creativity. I called my sister and told her how I felt. She admitted that she had also started crying on the way to the airport. I think we both would have been better off had we been willing to share those tears with each other before saying goodbye. Live and learn.

If you're like me, you prefer taking action over processing feelings. Despite all the work I've done over the years to embrace my emotions and communicate them in a healthy way, I still backslide on occasion. It's just more pleasant to let joy take the lead.

Taking Stock of Your Emotions

Remember the 2015 Disney-Pixar movie, *Inside Out*? It's a kid's movie, but it's worth watching no matter your age. It's about an eleven-year-old girl who experiences a major life-change when she and her family move halfway across the country. Riley isn't the main character, though. This story is about her core emotions: Joy, Sadness, Anger, Fear, and Disgust. Joy has been making all the major decisions so far, rarely letting any other emotion touch the control console inside Riley's head. But Joy and Sadness are swept into the recesses of Riley's mind, leaving Anger, Fear, and Disgust in charge. Riley steals her mom's credit card and tries to run away (back to her old home). During their adventure, Joy learns that Sadness has an important job in Riley's life. Sadness tells her, "Crying helps me slow down and obsess over the weight of life's problems." She helps Riley process the loss of her old friends which, in turn, leads Riley to hop off the bus at the last minute and return to her parents. Believe it or not, Anger, Fear, and Disgust have important jobs, too. In the end, the single-panel console that was formerly Joy's exclusive domain expands so that all the core emotions have a place to work. They work together to keep Riley healthy, safe, balanced, and yes, joyful (just not all the time).

Riley is a lovable, relatable example of the average human. Just like Riley, we have to make space for other emotions if we want to experience joy (a rare and intense form of happiness). And in order to process loss and grief, we have to make space for our tears, for our sadness. We must embrace all of our emotions, in a relatively even balance.

Explore Your Core Emotions

Take out your journal and list the five core emotions explored above: joy, sadness, anger, fear, and disgust. Think about recent moments in your life when you experienced each emotion. Next to each word, write a sentence or two about that moment. Where were you? What were you doing? Who were you with? Here's an example:

Recently I experienced pure joy when I took my daughter to the Pennsylvania Renaissance Faire and she met a mermaid. I stood next to her, watching not the mermaid somersaulting inside her sun-dappled tank, but my daughter. Her face was enraptured, lit up from within. She had one hand placed on the tank and the mermaid had pressed her palm to the same spot on the other side of the glass, as though they were touching. I was so happy in that moment, watching my daughter's magical experience.

Write a recent, personal example next to each emotion. Following the example, I want you to write the cues that let you know you were feeling this way. What did it feel like in your body? What thoughts went through your mind? How did you know you were experiencing that emotion? For example:

I was smiling as I watched my daughter. At first, I had no specific thoughts, as I was just enjoying the moment. Then I realized we had been standing there for a long time. I thought about her fascination and her innocence. I felt nostalgic for my own childhood, a feeling that settles itself in my belly, like a warm meal. I also felt delight in her delight, a feeling that starts in my heart, swells my chest, and spreads through my upper body. Most of all, I felt the tightness in my cheeks from smiling so broadly. I heard my own laughter and knew I was experiencing joy.

Be Aware of Your Feelings

Today's exercise is simple: Notice what you're feeling. As you move through your day, interacting with coworkers, family-members, and pets; taking phone calls and reading messages; making decisions big and small, just notice what you're feeling. Remember that "bad" is not a feeling. Neither is "okay," "fine," or "good." Use descriptive emotion-words: happy, sad, angry, scared, disgusted, surprised, etc.

Or look for nuanced words that give more information than the primary emotion. For example, happy may be a straightforward, accurate description of how you feel as you describe your ideal life, but hopeful, optimistic, and fulfilled might fill out the description. I was sad when my sister left for California, but I was also feeling nostalgic, loved, and lonely. When I noticed those feelings and communicated them to my sister—who returned the sentiment—I was able to get unstuck.

As you write about these intense, emotional moments in your life, you'll become more practiced at feeling and acknowledging emotions in real-time. Many people, especially folks who have experienced trauma, abandon the skill of articulating their feelings. We do this for good reason, as a defense against extreme pain and loss. But cutting ourselves off from emotion is an all-or-nothing endeavor. If we can't feel feelings, that means we avoid fear and sadness, but it also means we avoid joy and serenity. So practice writing about recent emotional experiences, articulating both the physical sensations and mental observations. This will help you explore your emotional landscape and learn to embrace your emotions in the moment.

Today's Act of Unconditional Self-Love

Call or visit someone close to your heart. Tell them how you feel about them, even if they already know. Use descriptive emotion words. (Check out the Worksheets section of this book for a little inspiration.)

Today's Journaling Prompts

1. How am I feeling today?

2. What physical sensations helped me realize what I'm feeling?
3. What specific thoughts came into my mind to help me understand what I'm feeling?
4. What circumstances led me to feel this way?

Day 6: Tackle Self-Doubt

Have you ever felt the painful twinge of self-doubt? The upset stomach, shallow breaths, and hot, flushed face: all tell-tale signs of a sudden drop in confidence. For some of us, it's a snide voice with a microphone inside our brains, batting down new ideas before they ever get off the ground. For others, it's a soft whisper, keeping us "safe" by gently refusing to let us take risks. Whatever your "self-doubt" sounds like, know that it's a perfectly normal experience.

Self-doubt is especially common when we're taking on a new challenge in life. Most of us have lost sleep the night before a big presentation, questioned our appearance, odor, and ability to talk before a first date, or wondered about our sanity as we submitted notice to quit one job and start a new one. Even in the therapy room, when my clients are reclining on the comfy chair with a hand tucked under Benji's "Pet Me" harness—a safe and comfortable environment—people experience the unfriendly bite of self-doubt. "Can my life really look like a miracle? How would I ever create that life? Do I even deserve it?" (Yes. You absolutely deserve it.)

You can address self-doubt with a number of techniques. I'm going to teach you four. The first one is "Challenging Negative Thinking," which is a cognitive behavioral therapy (CBT) technique. The second is "Small Victories," a technique that comes from animal-assisted therapy practices. The third is "Apple Core," a playful way of embracing your strengths inspired by a childhood prank. The last, but certainly not least, is "Supportive Character," which is drawn from narrative therapy.

Challenging Negative Thinking

Good, old-fashioned, evidence-based CBT techniques can challenge negative thinking and help you eliminate self-doubt. CBT is a well-researched, well-supported model that has helped thousands of people. Albert Ellis and Aaron T. Beck, psychologists active in the 1950s and 60s, respectively, developed the precursors to cognitive behavioral therapy. They believed that developing a negative view of the self would lead to a negative view of the world and one's future. They saw it as a feedback loop that could grow in either direction. In other words, a negative view of the world could lead to a negative view of self or vice versa. Albert Ellis identified the twelve most common irrational thoughts and suggested specific rational thoughts to use in place of them. CBT therapists have further developed this concept into "cognitive distortions" or "maladaptive thought patterns." If you can identify your go-to thought patterns, you can also identify ways to combat the negative thoughts. It's like your brain is an old dog set in its ways. CBT allows you to teach that old dog brain of yours new tricks.

What does this have to do with self-doubt? Well, it's likely that your self-doubt doesn't reflect the real picture. You probably express your self-doubt as a cognitive distortion (we all do it sometimes) and it fits into a negative loop that keeps you immersed in your problems. Your thoughts basically run in circles chasing their own tail (and tale) of self-doubt.

It might help to have an example: If you're getting ready for a first date and you notice a blemish on your skin, you might think,

"A zit?! I'm hideous. I might as well cancel this date. I'm going to die alone, surrounded by cats, and full of cheese." This is an example of "catastrophic thinking." Your rational brain knows that zits do not lead to a lonely death. Also, if you keep telling yourself you're hideous and will end up alone, chances are you won't agree to many dates. You may decide the world of romance is hideous, too. Your negative thoughts about yourself and the world get sucked into a painful loop that keeps you lonely and scared.

Here are the most common cognitive distortions:

1. Filtering: Focusing on a single negative detail and ignoring the rest of the situation.
2. Catastrophizing: Looking for the worst possible outcome in any negative situation.
3. Personalization: Assuming all comments and actions are personally directed at you or that you are the direct cause of a situation; attributing yourself as the cause of other people's actions.
4. Jumping to Conclusions: Assuming that you know what other people are thinking and feeling.
5. Fortune-Telling: Assuming that you know how the situation will turn out.
6. Emotional Reasoning: Assuming that if you feel this way, it must be true, even if the feeling is based in an unhealthy emotion.
7. "Should/Must/Ought" Statements: Making decisions based on a list of rules for how people should behave. When you violate your "should" rules, you feel guilty. When others violate your "should" rules, you feel angry. Albert Ellis called these statements "musterbation."

8. Polarized Thinking: Using an all-or-nothing mindset; approaching decisions with an either/or attitude.

9. Minimization: The other side of the catastrophizing coin: it refers to discounting or minimizing the positive situations in life.

10. Justification or Moral Licensing: Telling yourself it is okay to violate your standards or values because you're usually so good. For example, you make progress toward your goal of not stealing, so you reward yourself by lifting a candy bar.

Do any of these common maladaptive thought patterns seem familiar to you? If you catch yourself doing one or two of them on a consistent basis, you may be tempted to chastise yourself. STOP. DROP. ROLL AWAY FROM THE JUDGMENTS.

Seriously, don't judge yourself. There's a reason psychologists can list ten cognitive distortions and guarantee that most people will see themselves in the list. They are all extremely common. Remember the sociology lesson from Chapter One on Human Socialization? We're taught to think this way as children, and it is reinforced in hundreds of circumstances as we grow older. The point is not to judge or chastise yourself. Simply notice that you have a particular pattern of thinking. The more you notice it, the less it will happen. That may seem counterintuitive but trust me. If you want to kick-start the healing, you can give yourself a simple, rational mantra to combat the negative thought as it occurs. For example, "Catastro-phizing will get me nowhere. What's the rational truth?" Follow that thought with the rational truth about the situation: "It's true I have a zit, but I also have facial cleanser, a fancy new outfit, and a dazzling personality. This date will be fun."

Setting Yourself Up for Small Victories

Another technique for tackling self-doubt is an animal-assisted therapy exercise called "Small Victories." If you have a pet dog, you can do this at home. Even if you don't have a pet, animal rescues are always looking for volunteers to come play with their dogs. Benji often helps to soothe self-doubt by putting his utter trust and love in us, the humans in the room. It's a humbling experience to teach a dog a new trick and realize that he never doubted you for a second. The experience becomes empowering when we apply Small Victories to our human lives and realize we're not that different from Doggo.

Dogs learn best in small, manageable chunks. The handler has to remember three rules: break the task down into individual steps, treat the dog at exactly the right moment, and practice daily. The individual steps are simple, the treats are given immediately, and the daily practice rarely lasts for more than five minutes. So next time you doubt your ability to take on a new challenge, spend a little time with a dog, and remember, you don't have to wolf it all down at once. Teach them a new trick slowly and patiently, and then celebrate the abilities you're both mastering!

Teach a Dog to Sit:

1. Say your dog's name to make eye contact.
2. Show Doggo the treat. (They will follow it with their head, hoping to eat it.)
3. Hold the treat above your dog's head so they look up.
4. Starting at the nose, gently move the treat back, so Doggo has to move their head backwards.
5. Doggo will sit on the floor, in order to reach the treat. Say, "Sit," as this happens.
6. Immediately reward Doggo with the treat and lots of praise.

Teach a Dog to High-Five:

1. Instruct your dog to sit.
2. Gently tickle the back of their leg so they lift their paw.
3. As Doggo lifts their paw, say, "high-five."
4. Touch your hand to their raised paw.
5. Reward with a treat and lots of praise for completing the high-five.

As your dog is learning their new tricks, three things are happening for you. You get a rush of oxytocin (the love hormone) from the dog's big, round eyes and grateful snuggles. You also get a rush of dopamine from the excitement of success when Doggo learns the trick. Finally, you get a rush of motivation to break down whatever daunting task you're facing elsewhere in life using the Small Victories technique.

The Apple Core Activity

As the youngest of four children I was the butt of a great many jokes. My siblings would laughingly compare my spaghetti dinner to worms and then divide up the spoils when I left the table in tears. They would hide behind doors and leap out behind me shouting "braaains" like a *Night of the Living Dead* zombie. The silliest prank, primarily because I kept falling for it, was Apple Core. It's a pretty straightforward prank.

It goes like this: you eat an apple. Then, holding the gnawed apple core aloft, you shout to the room "APPLE CORE!" Someone else, probably an older brother, shouts back, "BALTIMORE!" You innocently ask them, "Who's Your Friend?!" And they point at the unsuspecting target and say "SHE IS!" Aw, isn't that sweet? Your friend—or ditzy little sister—probably feels really special when you choose her as the friend! But then you chuck the apple core directly at the ditzy little sister's noggin. Yep, throw it at her sweet, curly head because she fell for it again and forgot to duck. For my siblings and me, Apple Core evolved into a way of letting each other know "I love you, but you're obtuse." I offer you this sad glimpse into my youth because I want you to know I've felt your pain when you enter this next activity and inevitably get lobbed with an apple core.

This activity requires a solid, but ruthless friend. Or better yet, a sibling. It seems simple, but don't be deceived. You will probably get Apple Cored. Give your friend a pen, paper, and an apple core. Their job is to write down everything they hear. Your job is to list your strengths. Seems simple right? Before you get overly confident, you have to set a timer for five minutes. When the timer starts, you begin listing your many remarkable skills, talents, and special abilities. You may not stop until the timer sounds. If you start naming weaknesses instead of strengths, your friend gets to Apple Core you. If you begin downplaying your strengths, they get to Apple Core you. If you use the words "but", "besides", or "except," after any of your strengths... you guessed it. Apple Core. Finally, if you sputter out and say "I can't think of anymore" before the timer stops, say hello to the Apple Core. Your friend is there to keep you on track. Should they literally throw an apple core at you? Or is this just a metaphor? You decide. Just remember, the "core" lesson here is that you must learn to see all these remarkable strengths in yourself.

Many of us are blind to our strengths. That's why we dread this question in job interviews. I mentioned before how I wore a special pair of glasses that filtered out my strengths—the opposite of Benji's rose-colored puppy glasses. But an important part of developing self-love is removing those blinders. (Don't worry when those weaknesses inevitably slip into your list. They simply give you opportunities to practice self-compassion, a close friend of self-love.)

Everyone needs a friend so good they are willing to Apple Core us with affection. If, however, you don't feel like getting lobbed with an apple core, you could go online and do an assessment to better understand your strengths. There are a lot of boring tests online, so I went ahead and did the research for you. You can find a handful of my favorite assessments on www.annalisasmithson.com/tools. The Apple Core test may be more fun, but it's not exactly peer-reviewed research.

Here are some questions to get the juices flowing before the apple cores start flying:

- What do I do especially well?
- What comes easily or naturally to me?
- What kind of activities do I get lost in for hours?
- What parts of my job do I excel at?
- What do other people compliment me on?
- What am I proud of?

Accepting Kindness from a Supportive Character

A fourth way to tackle self-doubt is to use a narrative technique called "The Supportive Character." This technique can help you grow stronger in your self-confidence and self-love. It can empower you to take risks and overcome challenges despite self-doubt. It gives voice to the part of yourself that believes in you. It was developed by Jingwen Liu, M.Ed., a gifted therapist who specializes in feminist psychology and multicultural counseling.

Jingwen's client, Yu Yan, came to therapy with a history of severed attachments. Her parents had given her up for adoption, her best friend had moved to another city, and she had ended a romantic relationship that she had hoped would grow into marriage. A young woman in her early twenties, she had recently finished college. She was an avid reader, and without the shackles of homework assignments, she was happy to immerse herself in fiction. Introverts and bibliophiles can relate to Yu Yan's relief at escaping into a good book: "Sometimes I feel like my only friends are the characters in my books."

Yu Yan talked about her favorite novel, famous the world over: *Harry Potter and the Sorcerer's Stone.* Like Yu Yan, Harry Potter never knew his parents and had to create his own family. Yu Yan described the family that Harry gathered around himself, lingering on the kindness and wisdom of Albus Dumbledore. Her therapist, who, amazingly enough, has never read a Harry Potter novel, asked her, "What is it about this character, Dumbledore, that you feel drawn to?" Yu Yan talked about how supportive he is. "No matter how many mistakes Harry makes, Dumbledore always has gentle words for him; he shows so much love. I wish to have someone in my life like Dumbledore."

Struck by inspiration, Yu Yan's therapist asked her to join him in an experiment. "I want you to invite Dumbledore into the room.

Ask him to sit down with us and witness the problems that have brought you to therapy. Let him hear your story." Confused, but willing to follow her therapist's lead, Yu Yan talked to the fictional Dumbledore about her pain.

"Now give him a voice. Let him speak directly to you, as he would to Harry Potter." Yu Yan's self-doubt kept her silent for several long moments, but her therapist's kindness and support—not unlike the fictional Dumbledore's—gave her courage. "I think he would say that I have the strength inside me to overcome my pain. Make it a part of who I am. He would tell me that my character does not have to be defined by the people who hurt me. He would say, 'Yu Yan, you are enough.'" As Yu Yan gave voice to her wizardly father-figure, her own voice grew stronger. Now, whenever she begins to doubt herself, or gives her abusers too much power, she and her therapist invite Dumbledore into the room. His support and love are actually Yu Yan's self-support and self-love.

Imagine a supportive character in one of your favorite stories. Think about the personality traits that make them supportive to the hero. Allow yourself to be the hero of your own story and take this other person on as your supportive character. Have an imaginary conversation with them, and let them be kind to you. Accept their support and love fully, as if they are a real person. Know that this support and love are real. They come from a part of yourself that is stronger than your self-doubt.

Today's Act of Unconditional Self-Love

Do one of the things you identified earlier as a strength. For instance, if your answer to the question "What do I do especially well?" was "I make a mean chocolate cake," then the act of self-love should be to make a chocolate cake. Make it for yourself, or as a gift, or something to share with others—doesn't matter. Just embrace your strength or skill and do the thing without a shred of self-doubt.

Today's Journaling Prompts

1. What self-doubts do I carry every day?
2. Which of the techniques described in this chapter stand out to me the most? Which one would I like to try?
3. Which technique scares or intimidates me? Why?

Day 7: Explore Self-Love
Through Meditation

Have you ever imagined what a photograph of your brain might show? I love the idea of sticking my head inside an fMRI and spending an hour with a neuroscientist who can interpret the scan. I'm most curious about the changes in my brain before and after a meditation session. Experts have found varying data on exactly how meditation impacts different parts of the brain. But one thing is definite: meditation changes your brain. Neuroimaging studies have shown that it can improve self-regulation, help you become more focused in your problem-solving abilities, sharpen adaptive behavior, and increase your sense of interoception (the ability to sense what your body needs, such as hunger).[10] From a mental health perspective, we know that a daily meditation habit makes you more resilient to stress, calms the mind, and improves self-compassion.

Every morning at the clinic where Benji and I formerly facilitated groups for folks overcoming addiction, we would meditate. Our groups tried many different types of meditation: guided meditations from YouTube, classic meditations that we took turns reading aloud, soft music, or just a few minutes of silence. Benji was almost always in the room. And Benji was almost always acting-the-fool. We would only meditate for five to ten minutes, but those are the minutes that he preferred to play with his squeaker toy, explore people's lunches, and ask for belly scratches. At first, I had this inner monologue: "Benji, why can't you calm down?! Meditation is hard enough for beginners without having to block out your chewing sounds!" But Benji was oblivious to my inner critic (as he should be) and kept right on behaving as a puppy.

Group therapy can provide powerful healing opportunities and can inspire important changes in the participants' lives. I try to be mindful of my words and actions during group therapy, knowing that some folks look to my behavior to set the standard for the hour. So, every morning as our meditation began and Benji took advantage of our closed eyes to look for snacks, I had a decision to make. How would I handle this? Would I send him out of the room? Would I take his squeaker toy away to eliminate the distracting chewing sounds? Would I instruct him to "sit and stay" in embarrassed, ineffectual whispers?

One morning, I decided to try something different. I sat on the floor with Benji during the meditation. I removed his purple "Pet Me" harness and invited him to lay down next to me. I rested my hands on him and gave his head a scritch. He settled right down. I gently started petting him, moving my hand across him with each exhale, letting my breath calm us both. I noticed the softness of his ears and the coarseness of his ruff. I felt my mind wander for a moment as I noticed his scent and decided it was time for a bath. Then I brought my mind back to the moment with a smile. Even after all these years of meditating, my mind still wanders. And that's okay. My brain is supposed to produce thoughts—that's one of its jobs. In meditation, we notice the thought and come back to the breath. In this case, my breath brought me back to the rhythmic petting of the calm puppy. As the Honest Guy (an excellent YouTube channel for meditation) brought us out of his guided meditation, a lightbulb brightened for me. I could meditate with my pets!

What follows is a guided meditation that celebrates the presence of your pet—or animals in general—in your journey. Don't be surprised if your cat or dog comes into the room and gives you a nudge while you're doing this meditation. They may try to climb into your lap or invite you to play. Accept them, however they choose to involve themselves. While this is a written script, you may enjoy it more if a friend reads it aloud to you. To make it even more meaningful, the friend reading aloud can use the name of your pet. You can find recordings of this and other guided meditations on my website, annalisasmithson.com/tools.

Guided Meditation for Your Journey

Get your space set up by dimming the lights, lighting a scented candle, and perhaps burning an incense that you particularly enjoy. You might consider recording the following script into your smartphone so that you can fully immerse yourself in the experience as you play it back.

Sit or lie down in a comfortable position. Allow yourself to fully relax into your favorite spot and breathe in the familiar scents of home. Give yourself permission to fully immerse yourself in the journey you are about to take. If your pet wanders into the room, acknowledge them. Enjoy the sensation of their paws on your lap. Smile into their large, soulful eyes before closing your own. If they nudge your open hands, enjoy the softness of their fur and the wetness of their nose. Your pet is part of your heart and your home. They may wish to join you on this journey. With your eyes closed and your body relaxed, we will begin this guided meditation by counting down from 5...4...3...2...1...

You find yourself just inside the entryway to your own home. You are kneeling before the front door preparing for a journey. You are holding warm, fuzzy socks in your hand. They have a print that makes you smile as you pull them onto your feet. You relax a little more as you enjoy the sensation of the soft cloth against your toes. Perhaps you wiggle your toes and arch your feet to deepen the sensation. You lace up your boots and stand, stretching your calves and thighs as you pull yourself upright. You take in a full, deep belly breath, arching your back slightly. You realize you're holding an old, well-worn scarf that was a gift from someone you love. You continue smiling as you wrap the scarf around your neck and feel the warmth as though it is a hug from that same person. Your shoulders relax and your back settles into an easy, comfortable posture. You hear a jingle and look down to see your pet standing by your side. Your pet is happy, content just to be with you. As you clip a lead onto their collar, the sound gives you a sense of security. The texture of the leash in the palm of your hand is a comfort. The two of you are connected, stronger together.

Pause for a moment and breathe.

As you reach toward the doorknob to begin your journey, you notice a faint light seeping through the door frame. Slowly you turn the knob, sensing the brightening of the light. You open the door and you are fully absorbed in a brilliant white light. In this light, you find Love. Strength. Compassion. Your heart is illuminated and pure. Your pet is illuminated from within, adding a special purity to the already brilliant light. You pause to experience the moment, leaning into the light and relaxing further. Soon the light begins to fade. As it does, you realize that your higher power is with you on this journey. You are ready.

Pause for a moment and breathe.

You step through the door and find yourself in a wide, open field covered with flowers. You see deep orange, sunshine yellow, and rich burgundy. On the far edge of the clearing there are tall, majestic trees, still holding onto their colorful leaves. You are warm in your soft, cozy clothes, but you sense a cool nip in the air. You breathe deeply and smell the rich, spicy scent of the season. With your pet at your side, you set a slow, luxuriant pace. You enjoy the walk through the field, pausing occasionally to enjoy some of nature's treasures. You and your pet spy many treasures on the ground. You pick up a particular stone that catches your eye. For a moment you get lost in its beauty. What color is the stone? What is its texture? Is it cool or warm in your palm? You put the stone in your pocket and notice your pet has found a small, round object. It might be a walnut or an apple. They bat it around as if it's a ball, making small contented sounds, lost in the playful moment. When your pet notices you watching and smiling at their antics, they play even harder. They enjoy making you happy. Finally, your pet brings you the item. You place it in your pocket with your stone. You both received a treasure today.

Pause for a moment and breathe.

You and your pet reach the far side of the field and you step into the forest. The air feels cool and dry. The sound of crunching leaves beneath your feet momentarily distracts you. You look down and see that your footprints leave a faint glow in your wake. The brilliant light that blessed you in your home continues to illuminate your journey. You wish to move forward in your journey, but you are not yet sure how to enter the woods. Then you see two paths opening up before you. You pause to contemplate them. Your pet looks to you for guidance. Their trust in you gives you confidence. Unhurried, you study both paths. On your left is a cobblestone path, old and well-used, but clean and somehow familiar. The path to your right appears new. The dirt is recently packed, the brush clipped back just enough to allow you and your pet through. It is a little wild-looking. Both paths are appealing to your senses. You make your choice.

Pause for a moment and breathe.

As you wind your way down the chosen path, you notice that your pet has perked up their ears. Soon you begin to hear it, too. A faint hum. The hum resolves into voices. The voices sound cheerful—singing, talking, and laughing. You approach a small group of friendly people lounging around a campfire. They beckon you into the circle. Your pet tugs on a strap hanging down the side of your body. Your new friends are as curious as your pet. They ask you what it is you're carrying down the path that is so bulky and uncomfortable. You realize there is a large bag strapped to your back. You didn't even realize you were carrying this baggage. Something about this bag reminds you of the path you didn't choose. Your new friends offer to help you in setting it down. You place the bag on the ground and step back to observe it. It is yours, but only if you want it. As you inspect this baggage, you realize it is the only space in your surroundings not touched by your inner light. You reach into your pocket and wrap one hand around your new stone. Your pet nudges the bag away and you agree to let it go. Your capacity for self-compassion swells. Your new friends smile in agreement, supporting your choice. You bury your other hand in your pet's soft fur and feel grounded in their presence. You don't need that baggage. You are free to continue your journey with many new sources of strength. You say goodbye to your new friends and return to your chosen path.

Pause for a moment and breathe.

You and your pet follow the winding path to its far end, enjoying all it has to offer. You experience sights, sounds, and smells that delight your senses. You feel freer and lighter. You have more energy to enjoy your journey. Your pet appears buoyed by your new energy. Soon you are leaving the forest behind and returning to the familiar surroundings outside your home. You stand at the threshold of your home and contemplate your journey. The gifts you received. The choices you made. The companionship of your pet. You smile, pleased with your journey and strengthened by your companion. Your love for your pet has elevated your self-love. You step through the front door and return to the awareness of your physical body as I count down from 5...4...3...2...1...

Notice your hands and feet. Roll your wrists and ankles. Lift your shoulders slowly and roll your neck in a gentle circle. When you are ready, slowly and gently open your eyes. You may now end this guided meditation.

The Loving-Kindness Meditation

You probably have some familiarity with certain types of meditations. For instance, if you have ever completed a yoga class and enjoyed the 'savasana' pose at the end of the class, you have meditated. Perhaps you've even followed gurus like Deepak Chopra or downloaded an app like Headspace. But there are still many readers who are new to meditation. That's okay! You're never too old or too busy to try out meditation for the first time. There are many options, including mindfulness meditations, guided meditations, and body scan meditations, some of which I have included in this book. There are transcendental meditations and Qigong meditations, which are beyond the scope of this book. My favorite meditation, by far, is a classic Buddhist technique for increasing compassion for the world and the self. If you choose only one technique out of this book to incorporate into your life, let this be the one. Practicing a loving-kindness meditation every day is perhaps the quickest route to loving yourself as your dog loves you—unconditionally.

People often ask me, "How often do I need to meditate? And for how long?" I wish there were a prescription I could write for you:

"Meditate for ten minutes, twice daily" and that it would guarantee the feelings of serenity you are seeking. But the truth is, you meditate for as long as you need to, and as often as you need to, even if you're busy. A common saying goes, "You should sit in meditation for twenty minutes every day — unless you're too busy; then you should sit for an hour." You have spent many hours getting to know yourself as you have read this book. That knowledge and love that you are beginning to turn inward toward your authentic self can guide you. Let your authentic self answer the question, how much meditation do I need? As you spend more time mindfully exploring your life, your meditation practice will grow to suit your needs. And your brain will look like a masterpiece under that fMRI scan!

Consider recording this meditation into your smartphone, as well, and relax to the sound of your own voice offering you—and the world—the love we all so desperately need:

Begin by sitting comfortably in a quiet place. Take several long, slow breaths. Place one hand on your belly and one hand on your heart. Feel the rise and fall of your belly as you sink into a relaxed rhythm of breathing.

Close your eyes and think of your beloved pet. Perhaps they are truly sitting in your lap as you meditate, or perhaps you just imagine them in your mind's eye. Reflect on their unconditional love for you. Say aloud "May [say their name] be happy. May [name] be safe. May [name] be peaceful. May [name] be loved. May [name] be loving." Hold these compassionate feelings for your pet and enjoy the warmth it brings to your heart.

Now imagine yourself sitting in this room. Imagine yourself filled with the light of inner peace. See your authentic self in this image and then say aloud, "May I be happy. May I be safe. May I be peaceful. May I be loved. May I be loving." Enjoy the relaxed feeling for a few moments. Enjoy the feelings of happiness, safety, peace, and love.

Now shift your attention to someone in your inner circle. A beloved person who is close in friendship or family. Imagine them in your mind's eye and say aloud, "May [say their name] be happy. May [name] be safe. May [name] be peaceful. May [name] be loved. May [name] be loving." Embrace these compassionate feelings for your loved one.

Now think of a person one step out of your inner circle. This is a neutral person that you have no special feelings for, but you speak to occasionally. Perhaps a mail-carrier or bus-driver. Say aloud, "May [say their name] be happy. May [name] be safe. May [name] be peaceful. May [name] be loved. May [name] be loving." Hold these compassionate feelings for your fellow human and enjoy the warmth it brings into your heart.

Finally, imagine someone with whom you have a difficult time. This person may be hostile toward you and you may have painful feelings toward them. Try to hold their image as you say aloud, "May [say their name] be happy. May [name] be safe. May [name] be peaceful. May [name] be loved. May [name] be loving." Feel a little softer towards this difficult person.

As you complete your meditation, continue breathing deeply and rhythmically. Offer yourself gratitude for completing this meditation today.

A daily meditation practice will increase your feelings of self-compassion, self-acceptance, and self-love. Even if you feel restless or challenged at first, look for ways to gently incorporate meditation into your life. Start with 3 deep breaths once per day, then move on to a 3-minute guided practice, then a 5-minute practice. You might continue building on this or keep it short and low-pressure. Any little bit will help you learn to make space for—and ultimately to love—your authentic self.

Today's Act of Unconditional Self-Love

Find a guided loving-kindness meditation online and commit to trying it at least three times before finishing this book (or better yet, three times this week!) Three excellent sources (all accessible through YouTube) are WiseMindBody, The Honest Guys, and the University of New Hampshire's Health & Wellness Center. You can also access my recordings on annalisasmithson.com/tools.

Today's Journaling Prompts

1. What is loving-kindness to me?
2. How have I been kind to myself recently?
3. Why do I find it difficult to show myself loving-kindness?

Day 8: Play with Being Mindful

Where are you right now? As you read these words, take notice of where you are sitting. What does the seat feel like beneath your body? Is it hard or soft? Do you feel supported and comfortable? Are there any sounds around you? Any smells? Notice your surroundings.

Now look inward. As you read, do you have any new thoughts? Do you experience any new feelings? Perhaps you feel calm or content. Just by doing this, you are being mindful. You are practicing mindful reading. You can do any activity mindfully.

You might think, "Oh, I'm not into that mindfulness thing. I can't meditate. Yoga's not for me." Okay, all of that might have been true in the past, but you're working hard to make changes in your life. You're learning to love yourself authentically. That means your love is unconditional, your self-compassion is boundless, and your patience with your limitations is gentle and kind. So, ask your inner critic to give you a moment to read before dismissing your inner yogi. Both of them will benefit from a lesson in mindfulness.

What Is Mindfulness?

Mindfulness is a state of awareness. When you are fully engaged in something, participating actively with brain and body, you are being mindful. Rather than losing yourself in ruminations about the past or worries about the future, you focus fully on the present. Mindfulness lets you immerse yourself in the here-and-now, both in your surroundings, and within yourself.

As you incorporate more mindfulness into your daily living, you experience subtle but meaningful rewards. Mindfulness reduces the symptoms of anxiety (high blood pressure, stiff muscles, shaky legs, sweating) and enhances feelings of happiness and relaxation. It's almost unfair to call it a "technique" because it is truly just a way of being. Mindfulness is an unbiased, non-judgmental approach to living in the moment.

There is a difference between mindfulness and meditation. People often use the terms interchangeably. In fact, there is something called "mindfulness meditation" so the two clearly fit together somehow. But they are not the same thing. It can get confusing.

Being Aware

Recently I took my daughter, River, to the doctor for a wellness visit. After he looked her over and gave her a clean bill of health, I asked River, "Do you have any questions for Dr. Garcia? Anything about your body?" She surprised me by saying, "Yes!" She turned to the doctor and asked, "What does my heart look like?" I have no idea if conversations like this are typical. River is my only child, so I often just go with her flow and wonder later how "normal" we are. The doc seemed surprised, but he went with it. "Here, let me show you." He Googled "anatomy of the heart" and started teaching my curious kiddo about her body. "The heart is a muscle. It has to pump blood to the rest of your body. It pumps almost every second! Can you believe that? You've been in here for ten minutes and you didn't tell your heart to pump once, but it kept right on working.

Isn't that amazing?" Immersed in thoughts of mindfulness as I prepared to write this chapter, I thought, "You know? That *is* amazing." Our conscious mind isn't in charge of bodily systems like digestion, breathing, or circulating blood. But we can certainly impact those systems for better or worse. What would it be like to have awareness of my pumping heart all day long? Or just for ten minutes? Let's try it together.

Mindful Running

You may be familiar with mindful walking, the classic meditative activity. Jon Kabat-Zinn writes about this in his book, *Falling Awake: How to Practice Mindfulness in Everyday Life*. He clearly and simply describes the benefits of mindful walking, and a quick Google search will yield instructions on how to do it. If you have never tried mindful walking, I highly recommend it. But I was intrigued by River's conversation with Dr. Garcia and it inspired me to try something a little different: mindful running. I wanted to feel my heart pumping and practice mindfulness around this extraordinary part of my body. Here is the breakdown:

1. Lace up your best pair of running shoes and head outside for a jog. But here's the kicker—leave your headphones behind. That's right, runners, no music today. If Doggo is feeling up to it, you can mindfully grab their leash and bring them too.
2. Find a track or trail where you can run straight and true. No distractions or dangers such as cars passing. Avoid a place with tree roots or rocks to dodge.
3. Deliberately focus your attention on your feet as you begin your run. In mindful walking, the goal is to notice each part of the movement as it occurs. You might be instructed to

notice as you lift your foot, move your foot forward, place your heel on the ground, and shift your weight. After several conscious and purposeful movements, you pause for several normal breaths. With running, it feels a little different. It happens far more quickly and there is a slightly different set of instructions for your body. Mindful running looks like this:

1. Start by jogging slowly and take deliberate notice as you lift your foot.
2. Now feel the movement as you spread your toes.
3. Intentionally place your mid-sole on the ground.
4. Feel the shift of your weight forward as you roll through the toes.
5. Remember to breathe deeply and rhythmically. (Shallow breathing is a no-no when running.)

4. As you pick up your pace, the movements are happening much more quickly, so I use this phrase in my mind: "Lift, Spread, Sole (or Soul if you prefer), Breathe". Do this in rhythm with your steps.

5. While you're running, listen for your heart. This hard-working muscle is right there with you, fueling your movement with oxygen rich blood. Be mindful of how it feels in your body. Be grateful and gentle with it. Let the pounding of your chest set the pace for your mantra as you continue thinking, "Lift, Spread, Sole, Breath".

6. If your mind wanders, acknowledge it. Be okay with it. And then bring your mind back to your heart as you once again direct your body, "Lift, Spread, Sole, Breath". The mantra puts me in mind of a bird launching off a high branch to soar into the sky—or perhaps my own soul spreading its wings and ascending.

Try mindful running for ten minutes and then take inventory. What was it like? How do you feel? Any thoughts about your heart, your lungs, your feet? Your soul perhaps? Jot a few words in your journal.

Mindfulness in Daily Activities

You can practice mindfulness in any of your daily activities. This could be eating, washing your hands, hugging your partner, folding laundry, or petting the dog. Try it this morning as you prepare your coffee or tea. Breathe in the rich scent of the ground beans or dried leaves. Feel the warmth of the cup in the palms of your hands. Notice the wetness against your lips as you take the first sip. Enjoy the sensation of the liquid moving down your throat. Breathe deeply as you appreciate the aftertaste in your mouth. How do you feel after just a few minutes of a simple mindful activity?

Before I started enjoying the luxuries of the middle class and got myself a dishwasher, I used to wash my dishes by hand in the sink. For a long time, I dreaded the task. But when I started incorporating mindfulness into the experience, it became a chore I carried out willingly. Feeling the warm water flow over my skin, breathing in the sweet scent of soap, appreciating the shine of a clean glass, all of these are opportunities to be present in a surprisingly pleasant experience. It just took a deliberate shift in my thinking—or non-thinking. A rewiring of my thoughts, if you will. I learned to feel content while doing the dishes.

What is an activity that you find annoying or just repetitive? Is there a way to approach it mindfully? Can you make the chore work for you by incorporating it into your daily meditation habit? What would it be like to feel content with most of your daily life?

Mindfulness with Doggo

There is no better ambassador to a life of mindfulness than your pet. Spend an afternoon at the dog-park and you'll understand. (You'll also enjoy free entertainment and an ab workout from all the belly laughs. Dog-park politics are hilarious!) Dogs live fully in the present moment. When they find a fun toy, a smelly substance, or a crunchy snack (edible or not), they go all in. There are no thoughts about the past beyond instinctual safety measures. There are no thoughts of the future, period. They simply enjoy the toy, poop, or treat. Cats are also masters of the here-and-now. They curl up in your lap, inviting you to scritch their belly or pet their furry little heads, content to snuggle you, right up until they're not. Scratch, hiss, goodbye. They have no shame in using you for their here-and-now pleasure. Adorable little jerks.

Mindfulness with Doggo (or The Cat) asks you to let go of any distracting thoughts and follow your furry friend's lead. Grab their favorite toy—ball, frisbee, laser pointer, etc.—and play. That's it, just play. Lose yourself in the moment. Notice how their tail wags or twitches. Feel the texture of their fur when you touch them. Laugh at the wetness of their tongue if they give you a lick or a nibble. Use all your senses to be present with your pet. Simply put, experience mindfulness *of* doggo *with* doggo.

Mindfulness with Kiddo

That same principle—"Mindfulness with Doggo"—can be applied to your kiddo. Let yourself enjoy the moment with them next time they ask you to play. Jump into the pool and splash alongside them. Run through the field and give the soccer ball a kick. Deliberately employ your senses to experience the joy as fully as possible.

Sip some chocolate milk and savor the flavor as you pass the glass to your munchkin. Feel the cool milk on their warm skin as you wipe away their milk mustache. Breathe in the scent of their kiddie shampoo as you give a kiss on the head. Let their loud, unabashed laughter resonate in your own heart. Mindfulness can bring you to a new level of love, compassion, and joy if you let it. If you let go.

Progressive Muscle Relaxation Exercise

If you sometimes feel disconnected from your body—like your thoughts are so scattered or rapid that you just can't be present—there is another mindfulness exercise you can try. It is called Progressive Muscle Relaxation. This exercise is especially helpful for folks who experience anxiety, as the symptoms of anxiety often show up in the body. This exercise helps to soothe and relax the muscles simultaneously with the mind. Have someone read this section aloud for you, or go online and follow along to my recording: annalisasmithson.com/tools.

- Find a quiet place to sit comfortably. You may also lie down if that feels more natural. Unfold your arms and uncross your legs so you can move your muscles freely. Close your eyes if you wish, or if you prefer to keep your eyes open, simply soften your focus on the floor in front of you.
- Begin by taking a deep, full breath. Inhale for four counts. Hold the breath at the top. Then exhale for four counts. Pause at the bottom. Now take another, deep, full breath into your belly, this time for five counts. Hold at the top. Exhale for five counts, letting your belly deflate. Pause at the bottom. This next breath will be the deepest, most satisfying breath of your

day so far. Breathe in for six slow counts. Hold at the top. Open your mouth and sigh out the breath, making an "ahh" sound as you exhale.

- Now focus your attention on your feet. Curl your toes, feeling all ten of them. Now point them away from you, enjoying the tension in your ankles. Finally, flex them, allowing your arches to stretch fully. Relax your ankles with a gentle little roll as you continue breathing deeply.

- Bring your attention to your legs now. Tighten and tense the muscles in your thighs and calves. Place your palms on your legs and feel the muscles tightening from the outside in. You may notice a little shaking as you continue to tighten your muscles. Hold the tension for a few more moments. Now release the muscles and let all the tension fade. Breathe deeply as you observe the difference between the tension and the relaxation.

- Now tighten the muscles in your glutes. Let your sit bones shift as you tighten and tense the muscles all around your hips and buttocks. Hold the tension for a few moments. Then relax back into your chair. Breathe out and let all the tightness go.

- Focus on your stomach. Tighten up your stomach muscles, letting your back arch and your chest lift. Feel your entire trunk tense and tighten. Hold the tension for a few moments. Now exhale your breath in a full, relaxing motion as you release your stomach muscles.

- Arch your back and lift your chest once again as you tighten your shoulder blades. Let the muscles bunch across your back and feel the strength of your body. Tighten the muscles a little more and hold the tension. Hold it. Now relax. Let all the tension go. Relax into an easy posture and gently roll your shoulders.

- Now move the tension down into your arms. Tighten your upper arms, lower arms, and hands. Hold the tension as tightly as possible in your fists. Hold it until the muscles of your arms begin to tremble. Now relax. Release the tension and gently shake out your hands. Continue to breathe deeply.
- Finally, place your attention on your face. Scrunch your eyes closed. Wrinkle your nose. Press your tongue to the roof of your mouth. Tighten your cheeks. Make a funny face. Hold the tension in your facial muscles for a few moments. As you release the tension, soften your eyes once more and notice the relaxation in your chin, cheeks, and forehead. Take another deep breath.
- Continue your deep belly breathing, inhaling for six counts, pausing, and exhaling for six counts. Observe the relaxed feeling in the muscles of your entire body. Notice any lingering stiffness and try to relax further into those muscles. Continue breathing.
- Take any final movements, such as rolling your neck, shrugging your shoulders, stretching your arms, or pointing your toes.
- End this progressive muscle relaxation feeling relaxed and calm.

How do you feel? Try to locate the feeling in both your body and mind. Jump to the Worksheets section of this book and search the table of emotion words.

Getting Grounded

This grounding technique is especially useful when you are feeling overwhelmed. Sometimes anxiety and stress can take us out of our bodies and out of the present moment. Our thoughts begin to race, and we get caught up in worries, fears, or catastrophic thinking. This technique will bring you back to the present, into your body, and down to the literal ground.

- Take a seat. Place both feet on the ground. Place both hands palms down.
- Take a restorative breath. Begin speaking, slowly and deliberately.
- Say aloud five things you can see with your eyes.
- Say aloud four things you can hear with your ears.
- Say aloud three things you can touch with your hands or body.
- Say aloud two things you can smell with your nose.
- Say aloud one thing you can taste in your mouth.

Assess your feelings of being overwhelmed on a scale of one to ten. Wherever you land, can you be one point lower? Try the grounding technique again, this time even slower or more intentionally. How do you feel?

Today's Act of Unconditional Self-Love

Choose a mindfulness activity from this chapter to practice, or apply the practice of mindfulness to a favorite pastime in your day-to-day life. Be creative! The important part is that you attempt to be present and focused on the activity you choose.

Today's Journaling Prompts

1. Which mindfulness activity from this chapter stood out to me? Why?
2. How does my mind react when people talk about meditation, mindfulness, yoga, or similar activities? Why?
3. What was it like doing today's act of self-love? Was it easy, hard, comfortable, strange? How come?

Day 9: Forgive Yourself

Why should you forgive yourself? Because you deserve forgiveness, of course! As you deepen your practice of self-love, you will learn to believe that wholeheartedly. A simpler question for the moment is, how do we actually go through the process of forgiving ourselves? What steps do we take to forgive ourselves for the thousand tiny cuts we've inflicted on others and the handful of major transgressions we might make in our lives?

Hiding from Shame

It doesn't matter if the mistakes you're beating yourself up for are large or small. The steps to forgiveness are the same. We take the first step by not hiding from our mistakes. It is imperative to give a voice to that trifecta of painful emotions: guilt, shame, and blame. This is the fundamental step to forgiveness and carves a direct path to self-love. Recently, I had a session with a client that made the decision to take her first stride.

Elliott sat in front of her camera, crying silent tears at the start of our telehealth therapy session. I sat in front of my camera, respectfully averting my eyes to make space for her grief. Nobody likes to be gawped while they're crying. As seconds stretched into minutes, I pondered the cruelty of misplaced guilt. Guilt, shame, and blame are the prized winnings of our inner critic. They include a series of hurtful, usually illogical, thoughts that our inner critic spouts at us until we either accept these feelings as inevitable or make the choice to pivot. Elliott had just taken the courageous step of sharing the root of her trauma with me. She was ready to pivot.

Several years before, Elliott had lost a loved one to suicide. She had planned to see her best friend the night he took his life, but she never made the call, nor did she send a text. She spent almost 4 years carrying that burden. She blamed herself. She was ashamed of herself. She believed in her heart that she could have saved her friend, and she replayed 'what-ifs' on a loop in her mind. As her life moved forward she held herself back from embracing her accomplishments and realizing her joy. Each time she experienced a milestone, she reminded herself that her friend would never have those opportunities.

After a few well-meaning friends unwittingly dismissed her with platitudes like, "It's not your fault" and "How could you have known?" Elliott stuffed her feelings down. But the guilt, shame, and blame didn't go away, the feelings simply festered. Now, she was finally giving voice to those feelings and it was a painful process. Her journey into healing would be a long one, and while it would culminate in self-love, it had to begin with forgiveness.

Not everyone's guilt is born of such traumatic circumstances, but it doesn't have to be a deep trauma to cause damage. Each time we give the inner critic attention as it slings blame, we pull a little further away from self-love. Each time we hide our story of shame, we sink a little further into self-loathing. Dr. Brené Brown, shame researcher and author of *Rising Strong: How the ability to reset transforms the way we live, love, parent, and lead*, says, "to be forgiven is to be loved." Whether you're suffering a deep tragedy, or just beating yourself up for blaming your fart on the nerdy kid that one time in eighth grade, hiding from your feelings won't help. By acknowledging and giving voice to our stories of shame, by actually saying it out loud to an empathetic and objective person, we take the first step to forgiving ourselves. When we start talking about our younger selves and their many mistakes, we start seeing ourselves for what we really are: fallible humans.

My Shame Story

I grew up listening to my grandmother's stories about what it's like inside the mind of a writer. "When other folks drive past a big handsome house like that, they think, 'isn't that just a pretty ole house,' but when a writer goes past, someone like you or me, sugarlump, we think, 'I wonder who lives inside that house? I wonder what makes them laugh? I wonder what kinda scandals they been gettin' into." My writing doesn't do justice to her sassy Texan twang, but I hope you can hear the twinkle in her eye as you read her words.

Her playful, heartwarming newspaper column, "The Second Cup," inspired me to become an author. She told me soap-worthy stories about her first job at the "new hotel" in Wichita Falls, a place I imagined with gilded railings, luxurious pillows, and smartly dressed guests. When I left for college, her stories prompted me to take a job at a Clarion—decided less fancy but still fun. We exchanged handwritten letters talking about the shocking things I'd witnessed on third shift. I could picture her howling with laughter.

One weekend, I drove the torturous stretch of boring turnpike from Morgantown, WV to Morgantown, PA, looking forward to a long weekend with my besties. I arrived at my father's house on Thursday afternoon and looked across the field separating our homes. "I should go say hi to Grammom," I thought, "... nah, I'll be here all weekend. Plenty of time." I ignored my gut and put off my visit for another day. Sadly, another day never came. She died in her sleep that night. Grammom would have slapped my inner critic into next Tuesday if she could hear the kind of negative self-talk that followed her death. My guilt twisted into shame with words like "selfish" and "ungrateful." It took many months for me to find the courage to tell my sister my story of shame. Just by listening, she helped me let go of my misplaced guilt.

Learn from Mistakes

After giving your guilt, shame, and blame some air and sun, the next step to forgiveness is allowing yourself to grow from the experience. My sister, who never says goodbye without hugging and saying "I love you," helped me see that I had nothing to be ashamed of. There was still an opportunity to learn from my mistake. In her book, Rising Strong, Brown goes on to say, "So, forgiveness is not forgetting or walking away from accountability or condoning a hurtful act; it's the process of taking back and healing our lives so we can truly live." Self-forgiveness with accountability means that we are willing to learn from our experiences, learn from our mistakes.

My sister encouraged me to listen to my gut when it speaks and slow down for the people I love. I've learned to be present with my family when I can, and be kind to myself when I cannot.

My client Elliott also learned something in her vulnerability. Through painful exploration of her own grief, she acknowledged the albatross of her misplaced guilt and shame. By taking this first step, she was able to pivot and walk down the path of forgiveness. She finally saw that it's not fair to shoulder the responsibility for her friend's choice. By accepting his choice, she was able to forgive both herself and her friend.

Change the Narrative

The final step to forgiving yourself is to let go of the narrative. There's a loop playing over and over in your mind that asks "what if I did this" or "what if he said that" and "how could it be different." That narrative is designed by your inner critic to make you believe you made a shameful choice and it points your energy backward in your life. In his conversation with Oprah Winfrey on Super Soul Sunday, Bryan Stevenson, author of *Just Mercy*, said, "You are not the worst mistake you ever made. My clients have taught me that each person is more than the worst thing they've ever done because when I meet them, I meet them through some accusation. Something horrific and terrible, and what they teach me is that they're more than that crime, more than that worst act. I have come to believe that if someone tells a lie, they're not just a liar. If someone takes something that doesn't belong to them, they're not just a thief."

Whatever mistake you may or may not have made, it's okay to move forward. It's more than okay, it is kind, it is wise, it is an act of self-love. Allow yourself to focus your energy on the next chapter of your life instead of rereading the last.

Today's Act of Unconditional Self-Love

You know that story you've been agonizing over each night as you settle in to sleep? The one about how [negative, hurtful adjective] you are after making that same, damn mistake again? It's time to tell that story to someone else. This isn't a bitch session—it's a heart-to-heart conversation. Tell your confidant that you want to forgive yourself for a mistake you made and let them know how ready you are to take those steps. Even if your readiness is in the single digits of a 100-point ruler, it's still okay to have this heart-to-heart. Just be honest with yourself and your confidante. Finish the story by saying out loud, "I deserve to be forgiven."

Today's Journaling Prompts

1. What am I having a hard time forgiving myself for?
2. What are my patterns of self-blame?
3. What have I learned from my mistakes over the years?

Day 10: Love Yourself Like Your Dog Loves You

In an earlier chapter, you spent some time exploring your greatest accomplishments and strengths. I find that most people need a nudge or two to stay on the positive path during this exercise. During groups and workshops, I often find myself corralling the conversation back to our strengths, as people inevitably bond over their faux pas and failures. Why is it so easy to take that sharp left and start naming our weaknesses when asked about our strengths? Humility is certainly a virtue and I don't want to discourage it. However, I think there is a way to be both humble and authentic in our self-image—honoring both our areas of growth and our accomplishments.

I'd like to share the story of how I came to understand my strengths with the help of a therapy dog. But first, I'd like you to try the activity called "Letter from Doggo." You'll read my own letter from Doggo at the end of this chapter, but please don't skip to the end just yet.

If Doggo Could Talk…

Imagine that your pet—or one you have bonded with in the past—can talk. Try to embrace the animal's natural ability for unconditional love. Although most people think of dogs when we mention "unconditional love," I do believe other pets experience a similar bond with their humans. Cats like to play, snuggle, and offer a healing purr when their human needs them. I have a friend whose social work program keeps an emotional support iguana (ahem, I mean dragon) for their young and curious clients. Even fish like to swim to the front of the tank and give a watery hello when their human walks by. My point is that any bonded animal can take the role of singing your praises. You just have to let them. Now, grab a pen and paper, and let yourself speak on your pet's behalf.

- What would your pet say are your best qualities?
- What strengths does your pet see in you?
- Which of your accomplishments is your pet most proud of?

Write a Letter from Doggo

Letter-writing is a powerful therapeutic tool and you might be surprised at the immediate lift of your confidence as you complete this activity! This is actually one of my favorite activities after meeting a new client. Early in our work together, I invite my clients to write a letter from Benji (addressed to themselves) about how great it was to meet them. We do this together in session and make it as light and playful as possible; for example:

Dear Dominick,

It was great meeting you last week. When you threw my ball, I knew we would be good friends. You're a natural athlete and I'm not surprised you played football in college. Here are some of the other strengths I noticed in you....

With Unconditional Love,

Benji

P.S. I'm sorry I farted during your session. Please know that it will happen again. Probably today.

Try writing a letter of this nature from one of your critters. Address it to yourself, no matter how silly it feels. Be honest, loving, and authentic, just like your pet. Let yourself laugh or smile. Let yourself be warmed by the light shining through Doggo's rose-colored glasses. Don the playful puppy perspective. Notice how it feels to have someone else recognize your strengths and accomplishments. Put the letter someplace safe (like in your journal) and return to it whenever your inner critic starts talking trash on you.

Lessons We Learn from Animals

Now to return to my story. I wrote my own Letter from Doggo after the experience I'm about to share with you, but the dog in question wasn't Benji.

On my first day of work as a bonafide clinician, I had a meeting with my new clinical director to talk about my responsibilities, my boundaries, and my self-care. This is a critical conversation for all new clinicians. Self-care and boundaries are vitally important to the long-term success of our careers. My new director had a straightforward, no-bullshit way of addressing people and she half-jokingly informed me, "All the best therapists have a therapist." Despite her tone, I took her advice to heart and started looking for a personal therapist. It's not easy to find a good therapist! There are practical considerations like insurance, distance, and availability. There are clinical questions about their training and expertise. But most importantly, there's the therapeutic bond. Will I "click" with this person? It's hard to open up to someone if you don't click. Research supports this common-sense statement, as evidence points to the therapeutic alliance as one of the most important factors in positive counseling outcomes.[11]

After several test runs, I found my ideal therapist. If you've read my Psychology Today profile, you'll recognize this statement because my ideal therapist is a lot like my ideal client. She enjoys dogs, she has a sense of humor, and she embraces change. Enter Marcy Tocker, LPC, and Rosie the Pug, Therapy Doggo.

Marcy owns an animal sanctuary called Grey Muzzle Manor. She fosters senior dogs who would otherwise end up abandoned or euthanized. Senior pups don't often get second chances, but Grey Muzzle is this little slice of heaven with wide open green spaces, a pack of other animals to play with, and the medicine they need for warm, compassionate end-of-life care. The Manor is also home to horses, goats, pigs, chickens, cats, and occasional surprises like visiting ducks. It's a tranquil environment ideal for exploring one's mental and emotional health. But a tranquil environment isn't enough for it to be good therapy—you need a therapist for that. Our second or third session was in the early spring, still wet and chilly. I sludged through the mud and knocked on the cozy little trailer that overlooks the farm. This trailer is where Marcy sits and talks with clients when we're not in the field, visiting horses and pigs. Marcy pushed the door open with her foot, both arms bundled around a fidgety blanket.

"Hi, come on in," she said. "I need a few minutes before our session starts." Marcy looked a little frazzled, if I'm being honest.

"No problem, take your time." I knocked the mud off my boots and joined her inside. As I peeled off my jacket and got comfortable, I watched Marcy move around the room, arranging pillows on the floor and pushing furniture aside. She placed the fidgety blanket in the center of her makeshift playpen and waited. A snuffly little squish peeked through the bundle. I heard a goofy sound, part dog, part pig, and wondered what surprise critter Marcy had invited into her home today.

"This is Rosie," Marcy told me breathlessly. "We don't really have room for another foster right now, but I couldn't say no. Pugs are just so dear to my heart."

Rosie's human could no longer care for her. I don't know if they were moving, or bored, or what, but they begged Marcy to take her and she agreed. She didn't realize when she agreed that Rosie had some kind of cognitive problem. There was no mistaking the elderly nature of the pup. She had lumps all over her little body, her wrinkled pug nose had grown dry, her fur was patchy. She was no less than a million years old. But lots of senior dogs look rough despite their puppy brains that keep them young and playful until the very end. For Rosie it was different.

She snuffled around her little makeshift fence, weaving back and forth as she walked.

She bumped into a cushion and ping-ponged to the other side. Her anxiety was palpable. She was in a new environment, her humans were gone, and something was misfiring in her puppy brain. She felt scared and vulnerable. I could see the concern on Marcy's face, and I imagine I was seeing the tip of the iceberg; she's a professional counselor, which makes her a pro at regulating her emotions, especially when a client is in the room. Rosie's shuffling led her to my foot, and I leaned down to scratch her head. She gave my hand a push with her head, so I scooped her into my lap. Then she did something that was apparently remarkable. She spiraled once, stretched her body across my arm, pillowed my left hand, and fell fast asleep. I sat there awkwardly with my left arm extended under the dog. There would be no moving until Rosie was ready.

"I can't believe it," said Marcy. Her expression was nothing short of astonished. I still didn't understand the significance.

"What?" I asked.

"Rosie has been here for two days and she hasn't stopped moving once. She's been bouncing off furniture the entire time." Marcy was whispering now. "She's finally sleeping!" In quiet tones she explained her suspicions about Rosie's failing cognitive abilities. Physical ailments can be treated or at least made comfortable, but cognitive deficits in a senior dog indicate the end is coming. "Look at her," Marcy said. "She's so peaceful with you. What's it like for you?"

I looked down at the sweet little squish, snoring in my palm, and I let myself feel the moment. Sometimes when the emotional feels are quite strong, it's easier to start with baby steps, like the physical feelings. "My hand is warm, but also a little awkward. And that's okay. I like being her bed. Her peacefulness is contagious. I feel calmer now that she's settled down. I'm relieved she's not so scared and anxious now. I guess I feel... honored."

Rosie slept in my hand for the whole hour and when our session ended, I reluctantly handed her back to Marcy. She woke up and went back to the shuffling/weaving behaviors. I had given her the gift of a temporary peace, and she had given me a gift in return. For two weeks I held onto the feeling she had given me, savoring it. I journaled about it and took Rosie's lesson to heart. I even wrote a "letter from Doggo." When I returned to the farm two weeks later, I was excited to see Rosie again and to tell Marcy what I had learned from the experience. But the problem with loving a senior dog is that there's never enough time.

"She passed away a few days ago," Marcy told me gently, "I'm sorry."

My eyes filled with tears and I sat in silence for a few minutes. "I'm sorry, too," I said finally. It doesn't seem fair that dogs are with us for such a short time. They are such a special gift to the human race. I took a deep breath and decided to share my story with Marcy, despite the sudden shift from happiness to grief. She listened with her whole self, in that beautiful, healing way only a master therapist can offer. "I guess Rosie had one last lesson to teach before she died. She taught you not to doubt yourself," she said. "That's really special."

And she was right. You see, I had gone to therapy feeling upset and worried. I was doubting myself and my abilities. I wanted to be good at my job, but being a therapist is hard. Being a healer is hard. Rosie taught me that all the skills and techniques I had acquired were only extensions of the natural gift. I am a gifted healer. She brushed away my self-doubt when she found comfort simply by being in my presence. I processed the experience with Marcy, and I left feeling a mix of emotions: gratitude, sadness, nostalgia, acceptance, and peace. I planned to find my journal and write a second letter, this one from me to Rosie. Here are both letters.

A "letter from Doggo" on the day we met:

Dear Annalisa,

I'm so glad you came to the farm today. I was feeling quite poorly. You were so patient and calm while I explored the room. I think this must be one of your strengths. It really soothed my anxiety. And when I fell asleep in your arms you were very gentle and still. You must be an animal-lover to sit so still for me. You have the nature of a healer and a helper. I was able to relax and feel peace for the first time in days thanks to your healing nature. Don't ever doubt yourself as a therapist or as a mother.

With unconditional love,
Rosie the Pug, Therapy Doggo

A letter from me, on the day that I learned she had died:

Dear Rosie,

I'm so grateful that I had the chance to meet you. You're such a good dog and I hope you had a long and happy life before you became a Therapy Doggo on Marcy's farm. You taught me an important lesson about my strengths and my natural talents. I will hold that lesson in my heart. You are one of many beloved animals I plan to meet on the rainbow bridge. I only wish we had had more time.

With unconditional love,

Annalisa

Today's Act of Unconditional Self-Love

Snuggle your doggo (or cat or bunny or ferret or neighbor's dog).

Today's Journaling Prompts

1. What special ingredient do pets have in their heart to make unconditional love so natural for them?
2. What, exactly, is unconditional love?
3. When did I last offer myself compassion? What was going on in my life at that time?

Day 11: Get to Know Yourself

In the last chapter I described how Rosie the Pug helped me in therapy. It was a powerful and draining experience that ended in both smiles and tears. The journey to self-love is a roller coaster ride of emotional loops and turns. I left my sessions with Marcy clutching my journal, anxious to start a new entry. Writing is one of my primary self-care activities. And, boy, did I need self-care after that! What are your primary self-care activities? How do you take care of yourself?

In the next couple of chapters, you're going to get to know yourself a little better. You're going to learn about (and practice) self-care. Some self-care is universal—for example, everyone benefits from a good belly laugh. But most self-care is highly personalized. In order to make the most of the time and money you put into your self-care activities, you'll want to tailor the activities to your specific needs. Think of this chapter as a prereq for the more advanced self-care (and self-study) you'll do later on.

Self-care is such an important topic in mental health that I am dedicating three chapters to it. It is especially important in the early phases of mental health treatment. It can be difficult—and downright scary—to dive into our psyche. Many of us would prefer to avoid our problems as long as possible. So when it is time to face our problems, it can temporarily feel worse before it gets better. Knowing how to care for ourselves in those moments is a critical skill.

Journaling helps people process their feelings, make tough decisions, and feel more grounded. That's why it is a common suggestion for a self-care activity. But there are many options for self-care. Personally, I have a list of go-to activities that I use for self-care (which does include journaling) depending on what I need in the moment. What works for me won't necessarily work for you. It is important to do the work of exploring and articulating your personal forms of self-care. Without this foundational work, it will be a lot harder to care for yourself during and after life's challenges. What I'm getting at is the importance of self-awareness in self-care.

Quiz Your Way to Self-Awareness

Rather than relying on Google to trial and error your way through self-care activities, let's create more self-awareness. Self-awareness will help you discover and connect with your essential self. So, let's be analytical. It's not sexy, I know, but trust me. On annalisasmithson.com/tools you will find a series of tools that can help you get to know yourself better. If you loved taking quizzes on Myspace, Buzzfeed, or old Cosmo Magazines as a teen, you'll enjoy this activity!

Your Health

Take this healthy lifestyle quiz to assess how comfortable you are with your basic health needs. This includes how you sleep, what you eat, your use of cigarettes and other substances, and a few other key areas of healthy living. This should give you some ideas for how to establish or improve your basic physical self-care.

Stress Management

How do you perceive the stressors in your life? What tools do you use to cope with stressful situations? This test will give you insight into how you're already managing stress, and should give you some ideas for new methods to try. Practicing these methods will translate into realistic self-care when you're facing challenges.

Your Personality

Learning about your personality type (and the personality types of others) gives you insight into what makes you tick. What worries you, inspires you, motivates you to do better, and stifles you from growing. It's also fun to see how close to the mark these test-makers get! (They are well supported in studies.) And it's nice to feel understood.

Extroversion/Introversion

Extroversion/introversion isn't an either/or scenario. It's a scale or a spectrum, and you can land on it anywhere, which means you may actually be an ambivert. (Let's say you enjoy being alone with a book much of the time, but sometimes you feel more energized by taking your book to the cafe and chatting up the barista.) It's important to know where you sit on this scale. Learn about your tendencies and honor those needs accordingly.

Self-Care Analysis

Now that you know yourself a little better, I invite you to write up a self-care analysis.

- How do I recharge my batteries?

- When do I schedule "me" time?
- How do I communicate self-care boundaries?
- What area of my health do I excel at?
- What area of my health do I need to grow in?
- What is my go-to stress management skill?
- How do others with similar personality types do self-care?
- What does self-care look like for me now?
- What do I want it to look like in the future?

Today's Act of Unconditional Self-Love

It's time to indulge in some serious self-care. Identify a self-care ritual that you consciously or unconsciously lean on in times of stress. Maybe you like to lie in the grass staring at the night sky, or perhaps you're a candles-and-bubble-bath kind of person. If you don't have any self-care rituals, it's time to make one up and try it out for the first time.

Today's Journaling Prompts

1. What surprised me about the answers to some of the questions in this chapter?
2. What didn't surprise me, and how can I treat that in a positive light?
3. What am I afraid or ashamed to admit about myself that may not be that big of a deal after all?

Day 12: Create a Foundation of Self-Care

So before I ask, "How do you take care of yourself?" perhaps I should ask, "Do you—actually—take care of yourself?" If your answer is, "No, I do not practice self-care", then the most important lesson from this chapter is simply this: **Give yourself permission to invest a few minutes each day in doing things that fulfill you.** Many of us do not. American culture prizes "pulling yourself up by the bootstraps" and working independently to solve problems. We're not usually taught to ask for help. We're certainly not taught to prioritize our essential needs amongst the flurry of working weekends and abandoned vacation days. Self-care is seen as weak. We are taught that to be the alpha wolf we must sacrifice ourselves to the pack but, really, we need to care for ourselves to be able to care for the pack.

But here's a little secret. Good self-care actually makes you stronger. It makes you a more productive, happy, engaged worker. It makes you a more present and pleasant member of the family. It makes you *you* again.

But how do you feel when you try to take care of yourself? If words like unworthy, hesitant, or self-conscious come to mind, keep reading. It's very common for people to feel guilty about spending money and time on themselves. For many of us, it's like pulling teeth trying to convince ourselves that we deserve a simple treat. ("Don't waste the money, the calories," etc.). We have to talk ourselves into vacation days with phrases like, "Everyone deserves a day off every once in a while," or, "I'll come in early for a few days next week." Parents often believe that caring for others is the priority and self-care has to come last. If any of these behaviors sounds familiar, you haven't really nailed basic self-care yet.

Putting Yourself on Your To-Do List

Self-care isn't something you earn, like a treat for sitting or rolling over. It's something we all need to thrive. So, answer this: do you want to thrive? Do you want to model healthy, happy living for your kiddos and doggos? If so, Give Yourself Permission to Do Self-Care.

Why has "self-care" become such a buzzword these days? Seriously, it started trending on Google shortly after the 2016 presidential election, but according to the Merriam-Webster dictionary, its first recorded use was in 1841. We've been overworked and underpaid for a long time! Now more than ever, people are recognizing the need for self-care and searching for ways to practice it. You can go online and find thousands of ideas for self-care. Everything from bee-keeping to bungee-jumping can be a self-care activity.

Despite the abundance of ideas and the desire to engage, self-care often feels just out of reach of our self-made leash. We want to relax, destress, and recharge, but we still feel tethered to our problems and self-doubt. You may be short on time and money, but I want to challenge you to change your thoughts on self-care. Make it a priority in your life. Budget the money (if you plan on spending any— you don't have to) and give up a stressful activity in place of a self-care activity, thereby making the time. But more importantly than that, take your inspiration from the folks around you. Who in your life maintains a healthy balance of caring for others and caring for themselves? Let them be your guide in this next endeavor. Write the name of one or two "masters of self-care" in your life, then go talk to them. What do they do for self-care? How did they get to this point? What is their advice to you? With their help, and your permission, we're going to make you the next inspiration of self-care.

Speaking of which, Benji is a true master of great self-care. I love talking to my clients about the sweet, simple ways he models self-care for us. During therapy sessions and workshops, I often encourage people to notice the straightforward innocence of Benji's self-care and point out his activities. When he's hungry, he eats (and he doesn't count the calories). When he's stiff, he stretches (without criticizing his athletic abilities). When he's bored, he plays (and never feels self-conscious). He has a perfectly calibrated self-care barometer inside his puppy brain. Humans are similar to dogs in that we require fresh air, exercise, water, and sunshine every day in order to thrive, and we're most creative and relaxed after letting ourselves play. So, when Benji asks to go for a walk, I often invite my clients to walk with us, hand in paw. An outdoor therapy session may seem unconventional, but Benji's excellent modeling of self-care in the here-and-now is too inspiring to ignore.

Doggo's Self-Care Basics

Here are some foundational self-care ideas, inspired by Benji and other well-balanced individuals:

- Sleep (at night) until your body says "I'm good"
- Eat something nourishing
- Have safe sex (solo time counts too)
- Breathe in fresh air, preferably in a garden or grove of trees

- Connect with your higher power
- Create a safe, authentic connection with another human

Ever hear of Maslow's Hierarchy of Needs? It's okay if you haven't but you "need" to hear about it! In 1943, psychologist Abraham Maslow published a paper called "A Theory of Human Motivation." It states that we must meet our basic physiological and safety needs before we have the capacity and opportunity to focus on psychological, interpersonal, and creative needs. Like most aspects of being human, it's not an all-or-nothing situation. We can still create meaningful intimate relationships while struggling to find food and housing, but unmet basic needs will interfere in most other aspects of our lives. As we move up the hierarchy, fulfilling our needs for food, water, warmth, safety, and love, we come closer to "self-actualization." This is when we have leisure to engage in creative activities and realize our full potential. Most of the folks reading this book have already met their own basic needs—in the most obvious sense. You probably have a home, a cupboard full of groceries, and access to clean water.[12] But you mustn't neglect your actual health and well-being. Don't force yourself to run ragged caring for others before you attend to your own needs! You may have access to healthy food, cool water, and caring friends, but if you forget to partake in any of it, it doesn't count for much. It's like a dog that takes their prized bones, buries them, and forgets all about them! Consider what I'm saying. You are safe, secure, and have what you need to thrive. Give yourself permission to enjoy it. Fully attend to your basic human needs. Rest, eat, breathe, connect.

Today's Act of Unconditional Self-Love

The whole premise of this book suggests that you can and will love yourself like your dog loves you. It's time to let Doggo (or another loving pet) be your guide. Designate a decent chunk of time to slow down and find your zen. Let your pet take the lead. Follow them around the house and try emulating their kind of self-care. You might find yourself drinking a cool glass of water, wandering through the yard smelling flowers, or napping in a patch of sunlight. Embrace it!

Today's Journaling Prompts

1. What are my basic needs? What needs have I been putting ahead of others and why?
2. What was it like to find my zen with my pet? What did I learn about myself?

Day 13: Practice Whole Self-Care

You are probably quite good at certain types of self-care—when you give yourself permission to indulge. But did you know there are multiple domains of self-care? Let's explore the four primary domains and select a few examples from each that fit your style.

But first, a point to remember: self-care isn't escapism (at least not entirely).

Some self-care activities will help you escape from the stressors in your life for a period of time. They give you space from your problems—a little more length on your leash, so to speak. They give you the opportunity to balance yourself, recharge your batteries, and find where you buried your favorite bones. In order to return to the problems later and feel confident enough to solve them, you need to make time for self-care. In other words, taking a temporary distraction from your stressors can be helpful. Just be careful you don't fall down the rabbit hole of habitually avoiding your problems. You want to aim for a healthy, temporary distraction, rather than an unhealthy, bound-to-fail pattern of avoidance. Now let's explore the four domains. They are:

- Physical Self-Care
- Cognitive Self-Care

- Emotional Self-Care
- Realistic Self-Care

Let's jump right in.

Physical Self-Care

Have you ever experienced a runner's high? That moment, about seven or eight minutes into your jog, when everything just clicks into place. You experience a brief, beautiful sense of euphoria. Cramps disappear, side-stitches ease, your breathing becomes deeper, faster, and more fulfilling. You feel like you're sailing along the trail and you remember how much you love running. It's a real thing and it isn't limited to running. A "runner's high" can happen when you're swimming, biking, or even taking Doggo on a long walk. When you do something that gets your blood pumping and your oxygen flowing, your brain releases feel-good hormones called endorphins. These are natural painkillers that your brain controls and your activity can trigger. They may be part of the reason exercise feels so damn good. Scientists have also suggested that norepinephrine secretion, dopamine, or serotonin could be the neurotransmitters that give us such a good time during exercise. Whatever the mechanism, it's an accepted fact that long, rhythmic aerobics create opportunities for the brain to counter the effects of stress and anxiety.

Jada Rohner, certified dance and fitness instructor, explains the impact of exercise on stress: "When our bodies function better, our minds are more at ease. Rigorous exercise releases endorphins which make people feel like they are on a natural high. Runners and dancers often speak of this effect after a great workout. Cardiovascular aerobic exercise boosts our energy and makes us feel like we are more motivated to get through our daily routine. Those who practice yoga or Pilates speak of a similar effect, but they use words like 'calming' and 'centering.'"

Rohner describes other physiological benefits of exercise, such as the oxygenation of blood, the release of serotonin during deep belly breathing, and the easing of tensed muscles from simple stretches such as neck and shoulder rolls. Think about it: scrunching your face, grinding your teeth, and tightening your neck and shoulders are probably a few things you unknowingly do whenever you experience stress. Some of these involuntary expressions of stress can lead to migraines, back pain, and ultimately even more discomfort and stress.

As Rohner says, "For many, myself included, the simple act of exercise is the ultimate form of self-care. We can put down whatever is causing us stress for an hour or so. We can clear our heads for a time and release the stress from our bodies in a healthy way. This allows us to recharge mentally and look at whatever is causing us stress in a new and sometimes more effective way."

So how will you incorporate physical self-care into your daily life? You could play a competitive sport, try hot yoga, dance like a toddler, or strap on some roller skates. You could swim across the lake and even take some time to splash, just for fun. You could simply stretch at the beginning and end of each day. And—how could I forget?—you could walk your dog! Whatever physical self-care you choose, try to have some fun with it! Grab your journal and write about some of the physical activities you enjoy:

- When you have been stressed in the past, what kind of physical activities gave you release?
- Do you enjoy solo exercise, a class-like setting, or full-on competitive sports?

- What was the last physical activity that left you feeling focused and energized? (For me, it was paddle-boarding!)

Cognitive Self-Care

Cognitive self-care is just a fancy way of saying you need a "brain break." (My daughter tells me that's what they call it in elementary school.) It includes any activity that engages and focuses the mind, thereby taking your attention away from the thing causing you stress (such as common core math). The goal is to offer up your energy to your intellectual and/or creative self. Instead of ruminating on your problems, you force the problem to "sit and stay" for a time. It's amazing how often a solution to the problem occurs to you while you're on a "brain break."

One of the best examples of cognitive self-care is guided meditation. A daily meditation habit is second only to sleep for rejuvenation and good health. You learned about the science of meditation in an earlier chapter. Continue investing in yourself with five minutes per day of guided meditation because that will precipitate incredible growth. Your ability to maintain serenity in the face of stress may well astonish you. Like a flower being nurtured every day with a cool drink of water, your cognitive abilities will blossom.

Other examples of cognitive self-care include working on a jigsaw puzzle, or doing sudoku, mahjong, or even a simple word-find. A more creative approach might be knitting, painting, or sculpting. In my group therapy room at the clinic, I kept a constantly evolving list of art-based therapeutic activities along with the corresponding materials. The shelves were lined with everything from adult coloring books to an old, well-loved guitar. People spent hours in that room crafting and creating, all the while noticing their thoughts, feelings, and any decisions that bubbled to the surface.

As a self-proclaimed bibliophile, my favorite types of self-care involve the written word. Losing myself in some fantasy fiction (I rarely aim for thought-provoking when the goal is self-care) is the fastest route to relaxation for me. And as an ambivert, I love the fact that reading is a portable self-care activity. I can take my latest novel to the local bookstore/cafe and be surrounded by other bibliophiles. I can also disappear into the woods with a backpack full of snacks and paperbacks. Either way, my ambivert self can find some TLC with a good book.

A word about television. My favorite professor, who later became my mentor and one of the best humans I have ever known, rather callously announced to my cohort once that "watching television doesn't count as self-care!" We were outraged. "But, Dr. Farrell!" I spluttered, "What about *Star Trek*?!" As a fellow Trekkie, surely he understood the exception to the rule. I could accept *South Park* and *Real Housewives* as outside the realm of self-care, but *Star Trek*? The show that taught us "that humanity will reach maturity and wisdom on the day it begins not just to tolerate, but take a special delight in differences in ideas..."? (Thank you, Gene Roddenberry.) Rarely do I feel cozier than when I'm curled up with my pets and a cuppa hot tea, watching reruns of *Next Generation*. But Dr. Farrell was insistent. "You know I love *Star Trek*. But no, even that. TV doesn't count as self-care." It pains me to echo this sentiment, but he was probably right. Watching television can be fun and relaxing, but a daily TV habit won't give you anywhere near the benefits of a daily meditation or reading habit.[13] Grab your journal, and give the following questions some thought:

- What is your favorite type of brain-break?
- Were you surprised by any of the cognitive self-care activities listed?

• Which cognitive self-care activities could fit in with the recommended hobbies for your personality type?

Emotional Self-Care

No matter what your personality type or where you land on the introversion scale, emotional self-care is critically important. Healthy boundaries and quality alone time are more than just a treat for introverts and bookworms; they are an exceptionally important aspect of emotional self-care. Remember that humans are social creatures. All of us occasionally need a shoulder to cry on, a hand (or paw) to hold, and a great big belly laugh. We need to process our feelings, out loud and with an empathetic person. So please, don't make all your emotional self-care activities solo activities. Allow yourself to ask for help—or company—when you need it.

Emotional self-care activities might include journaling, calling a friend, seeing a therapist, writing a gratitude list, or practicing compassionate self-talk. Try to nurture your feelings without judgment. It's hard enough to process feelings of anger or sadness. Don't fall into the trap of telling yourself you should or shouldn't feel something. Effective emotional self-care can also happen when you nurture someone else's feelings. Helping others is often a path to healing ourselves. Practice active listening with someone you love and consider asking someone you love to actively listen to you. Check out the Worksheets section of this book for tips on how to be a better listener.

Here is a simple, straightforward way to practice emotional self-care. The next time someone gives you a compliment, accept the compliment. If you notice your inner critic objecting, downplaying, or dismissing the compliment, give your critic a double helping of your middle finger. Accept the compliment with a thank-you and make a note of it in your journal for good measure. I'm 100 percent sure you deserve the compliment, whatever it turns out to be. Because you're fabulous.

In addition to your loved ones, lean on your pets to help you practice emotional self-care. That is, after all, the premise of this book. Doggo loves you unconditionally and you fully deserve such love. One of my favorite meditations is by Deepak Chopra, published on YouTube by the Chopra Center. It is called "Living Carefree" and it always helps me feel lighthearted. Every time I share it with colleagues or clients, I wait for the inevitable chuckle when Dr. Chopra tells the listener to "pet your cat" around the three-minute mark. But it's worth remembering. Sitting quietly with a purring cat can make you feel so loved and so loving. This is excellent emotional self-care. Dr. Chopra has other insights for emotional self-care in this particular meditation. He says, "Practice living each moment as it comes, with a light and open heart, and pay attention to how those carefree moments carry with them greater abundance and boundless joy. To help you do this, take some time to reflect on good times. Look at old photos. Play a favorite song. Pet your cat. Take a leisurely walk. Or spend time with someone who warms your heart. Experience the joy of all you love—including yourself."

There are moments when emotional self-care requires us to say to another person, "I'm not okay." I remember the day Benji was diagnosed with epilepsy. I was terrified. Before we knew for sure what was happening, I was getting sucked into a maladaptive loop of catastrophic thinking. I had to go to work alone for the first time in months while Benji was at the neurologist with my partner. I was standing at the front door, keys in hand, looking at Benji looking at me. I'm sure he was wondering why he wasn't coming. Dogs are sensitive to routines and doubly sensitive to their human's feelings. My feelings were overwhelming that day. I looked at Benji and thought about saying, "Everything's going to be okay, buddy." But the truth is, I wasn't sure everything would be okay. So instead I knelt down, wrapped my arms around him, and said, "Benji, I'm scared." He gently pulled out of my hug (dogs don't like hugs), turned 180 degrees, and backed his truck up directly onto my lap. I smiled through my tears as he leaned against me in what I chose to interpret as Doggo language for "I'm here for you." By naming my fear, I started to feel some emotional relief. I was able to go to work and focus on my tasks while awaiting the call from my partner. Benji is fine, by the way. He takes his medication wrapped in snacks, to his daily delight, which minimize the severity and frequency of his seizures. His veterinarian is a brilliant, caring person who has helped ensure that Benji continues to lead a happy, healthy life. And Benji continues to be a brilliant, caring puppy that helps me lead a happy, healthy life. Three cheers for Benji and the good doctor!

Here are some questions to get you thinking about emotional self-care:

- How do you typically take care of your emotional needs?
- Who could you lean on when you need a hand to hold or a shoulder for your tears?
- Name one solo activity and another interpersonal activity that could provide for your emotional self-care.

Realistic Self-Care

So far, we have been exploring self-care activities that help you disconnect from the stressors in your life. Escapism or distraction work for a time, but there is another domain of self-care that may be even more useful for you. Realistic self-care helps you face your stressors head-on with carefully thought-out activities. These activities should be aimed at resolving the stressors in your life one small step at a time. Harnessing up your dog sled team and mushing toward the finish line looks like a flurry of stress from the sidelines...but if you're doing it to resolve the stressor, then it, too, counts as self-care.

Consider writing a realistic, time-bound to-do list (with brain-breaks and essential self-care included) aimed at resolving and eliminating a stressor in your life. For example, perhaps you're feeling anxious about an upcoming deadline—let's say April 15. You know you need to prepare your taxes, but you're procrastinating. (It's possible this is an emotion-regulation problem rather than an actual time-management problem. Don't be too hard on yourself. Lots of people feel scared and anxious about their finances.) A realistic, time-bound to-do list for solving this problem might look like this:

- Today, I will search online for three local tax experts and select my favorite
- Tonight, I will go to sleep early and get eight hours of rest
- Tomorrow, I will contact the tax expert and make an appointment
- By the end of this week, I will collect my proof of income and expense documents
- This weekend, I will disconnect by reading a trashy, non-tax-related romance novel
- Next week, I will attend my tax appointment
- By the end of next week, I will mail the check/tax documents to Uncle Sam
- Next weekend, I will reward myself by going paddle-boarding

Sometimes I start with a to-do item that I've already completed, just so I can feel the satisfaction of crossing it off the list.

Other examples of realistic self-care might include taking a lunch break, turning off your cell phone, avoiding the snooze button (yes that would mean getting up early), or accepting a messy house just the way it is.

Another way of doing realistic self-care is learning to say no when people ask you to heap more onto your plate. Sometimes you have to stop and assess your current schedule and actually give yourself permission to say no *before* the next project comes along. It can be painful. We don't want to disappoint our family, appear lazy to our boss, or let anyone down. But at times it is absolutely necessary to say no. Think of it as guarding your favorite chew toy from the other neighborhood dogs, except that chew toy is your set of healthy boundaries. You've worked so hard to experience self-love and practice self-care. Let yourself continue these great habits by saying no to the world once in a while.

Today's Act of Unconditional Self Love

Do one of your self-care activities, of course! During your self-care activity I want you to use the mindfulness technique, *Thinking-Feeling-Deciding*. It goes like this: While you're caring for yourself, take note of any thoughts that pop into your head. Consciously notice any feelings that follow your thoughts. Then ask yourself, "What am I deciding to do because of these thoughts and feelings?" Be mindful and enjoy yourself!

Today's Journaling Prompts

1. Which type of self-care works best for me? Why?
2. What new self-care activities will I give myself permission to try?

Day 14: Explore Your Values

Values help us define what is important to us. They are part of our core belief system. They determine what matters to us within our culture, within ourselves, and in each "life domain." They guide us in making ethical, authentic decisions. When our choices honor our values, we tend to feel fulfilled, happy, and successful. When we make decisions that are not informed by our values, we tend to feel unfulfilled and uncomfortable. Stress and sometimes even anxiety can grow from this state. It might help to have an example.

My former client, Jo, whom you met in an earlier chapter, continued working with me for several years. When she first contacted me, her goal was simple (but not easy): to stop drinking alcohol. Week after week she would come to me in tears, explaining how she had "slipped up" over the weekend, but had determined not to let it happen again. She was certain that if she could muster enough willpower, she would get sober. She did everything right: she went to AA meetings, identified her triggers for drinking, eliminated the most dangerous "people, places, and things" that would lead her back to the bottle—and yet every few weeks or months, she would pick up again. I wondered whether, perhaps, we were focusing on the wrong goals. I wanted to follow her lead, of course, and honor her desire to quit drinking as a major life goal. But perhaps there was more to it. I invited her to complete a values exploration exercise in hopes of discovering what we were missing. It proved very useful for both her sobriety and her expanded personal growth goals. Here it is:

Five Steps to Figure Out Your Values

Step One: Think of someone that inspires you. It could be a family member, a public figure, someone from your youth, or even a fictional character. What are some things you admire about them? Jo selected her grandmother. She told me about a time from her youth when she lived with her grandmother. She said, "My grandmother was always just herself, no matter what other people said or thought. She would wear these ridiculous sweatshirts for every holiday, and I hated them then, but now I love how she was just herself. She was just so full of life. She was always looking for a reason to celebrate. And she loved me so much."

Step Two: Identify that person's values. Jo was drawn to her grandmother's authenticity, her confidence, perhaps her playfulness and sense of fun. She also identified "love," which is a core value for most of us. If you respect these values in someone else, it's usually a clue about what you value within yourself. That said, you don't always have to share the same values as the person who inspires you. There are hundreds of possible values to choose from.

Step Three: Have a real or imagined conversation with the person you admire. Ask them, "What are your core values?" and "What do you think my values are?" Jo had a hard time with this step. She said, "My grandmother always thought the best of me. She would say I'm kind and generous, smart and patient. But she didn't see the real me." Perhaps it's true that Jo isn't as angelic as her grandmother believed, but it's also true that our heroes—particularly childhood heroes—shape our values.

Step Four: Start by writing five to ten values that you try to live by. Spend a few minutes coming up with them on your own. After you've exhausted your own vocabulary of values, go to the Worksheets section of this book and look over my list. You might be surprised by some of the words that jump out at you. Jo came up with seven values that she was already incorporating into her daily life, and another five that she wanted to embrace, but wasn't sure how. Not surprisingly, several of her grandmother's values appeared on the list, including *love* and *fun*. Her grandmother's rose-colored beliefs about Jo also made their way onto the list. (Remember Benji's rose-tinted glasses that let him love me and all his other humans unconditionally?) *Generosity* and *patience* are values she wanted to honor going forward. She also named a few that she found confusing. "I used to care a lot more about being *successful* and making *money*. I still care—I don't want to be broke. But it's different now." Our values can change as we grow older and our circumstances change. It's okay to let go of values that once served us, but no longer fit into our lives. Sometimes we outgrow our values, like how some dogs outgrow being lap dogs (despite some earnest and leg-crushing attempts).

Step Five: Practice talking about your values. Approach two or three people that you respect and invite them into a conversation about values. You may need to tell your people about the concept, as usually only therapists want to talk about things like values and "articulating your authentic self." By teaching your friends about this concept, and by learning about your friends' values, your own values begin to emerge.

Sometimes you'll begin to see how your actions complement or clash with your values. These lightbulb moments are really special, like when another of my clients said, "When I was a little kid, I wanted to be an astronaut. I always loved lying in my backyard and staring at the stars. I would imagine exploring faraway planets and meeting aliens. I realize now that *adventure* is one of my core values. I became a homebody after I got married, but I still truly value adventure!"

After Jo spent some time reconnecting with the memory of her grandmother, she was able to articulate not only what she values, but what she doesn't value. What doesn't work for her anymore. She started noticing how much time and energy she gave to activities and ideals that she doesn't value. Then her life started to change. I asked her to make a conscious, intentional effort to honor her values each day. She would write in her journal "Today I honored my values by doing the following activities..." She started off small, like calling an old friend or giving herself permission to go to bed early, and then built up a series of healthy habits that slowly took the place of her old habits. It was a long and difficult process, but with intention and self-compassion she did it!

Today's Act of Unconditional Self-Love

After you've completed the prompts below, do something that honors your values. For example, if *family* is one of your core values, invite a beloved family member out for ice cream; or if *love* is a core value, write a love note/song/poem to someone you care about.

Today's Journaling Prompts

1. What are my values?
2. Where do my values come from?
3. Whom do I admire and what are their values?
4. How have my values changed? (What we valued as children and young adults naturally changes as we develop.)

Day 15: Set Values-Based Goals

Now that you can fully articulate your values, it's time to set some goals. I started this process with my career counselor, Cori, many years ago (before I became a therapist) and it changed me. Being able to talk about my values helps me make decisions that fit my life and needs. If you think of your values as a compass, guiding your journey through life, you can see that a value isn't something you achieve. It is a part of your inner GPS, something that we hardwire into our daily lives, and ultimately into our journey. I have seven core values that I try to honor in small ways throughout my daily life:

- Joy (my centering value)
- Family
- Prosperity
- Service
- Knowledge
- Health
- Adventure
- Nature/animals

Goals are part of the journey. If values are the compass showing you the direction you need to take, goals are the landmarks you pass along the way. The goal doesn't have to be a massive mountain you're attempting to climb, either. You can create small, manageable peaks that you climb in your own time. Don't worry if you have a hard time setting values-based goals at first. When I tried doing this the first time, I needed a bit of handholding from my counselor. My first attempt looked like this:

The value: to be happy
The goal: to do things that make me happy every day

After hearing this, my counselor smiled and picked up a dry-erase marker. In a curious but gentle voice, she asked "What does 'being happy' look like?" I can answer that question readily, but only because she guided me through an art therapy intervention to help me explore exactly that. (At the time, it was a crushing question. My inner dialogue started jibbering: What *does* "being happy" look like? Am I actually happy? Am I fooling myself? Should I Google it? Okay, don't panic.) Thanks to therapy, I now know what being happy looks like for me: I feel most content—and often joyful—when I am in the woods, surrounded by family and friends. I'm snuggling my dog in front of a bright, warm campfire. My muscles have that good-sore feeling from hiking all afternoon and there's a stack of books next to the hammock, waiting for my early morning alone time. Cori had written several words on the whiteboard while I talked, words that were eventually honed into the seven core values I listed above. I realized when I honor the other six values in my daily life, I experience joy. We marked that as my "centering value" and I decided to incorporate the Buddhist teachings of equanimity in my life. I let go of the idea of "achieving happiness" and let it exist on its own in my life.

Getting SMART About Your Goals

Cori then explained a concept that many are familiar with: SMART goals. "Let's get more specific about what kinds of things bring you joy, maybe from somewhere else in your list," she suggested. We focused on family. "What about 'family' is important or valuable to you?" Cori asked me. As the picture of us around a campfire became clearer, my goals started to write themselves. Cori taught me to create goals that not only fit my values, but are also:

Specific
Measurable
Achievable
Realistic
Time-Bound

My next attempt at writing values-based goals looked like this:

The value: Spending quality time with my family
The goal: Arrange a family camping trip next summer

Since it was October, she asked me to get more achievable and realistic in the short-term. She also asked me to be specific about who I'm including in my family or "framily" as my LGBTQ community often calls it.

My final result looked like this:
The value: Spending quality time with my family

The goals: Set a recurring reminder in my phone before I leave counseling today to call my parents during my Monday commutes. Invite my best friend and her family on a fall hike next weekend (and go alone if they are busy). Send out the save-the-date for next summer's camping trip before the end of October.

Cori applauded my final attempt and explained that in addition to being specific, achievable, and realistic, these are truly measurable and time-bound goals. By attaching a time-frame and a clear set of actions to each goal, we had the tools we needed to determine how successful I had been at accomplishing each goal. All of the goals were thoughtfully identified to nurture my family values. I copied the values and goals into my journal and we came back to them several times over the course of counseling.

Values Are Your Compass, Goals Are Your Landmarks

One last note before you try it. Why do we talk about values-based goals, rather than just goals? It's an important distinction. When we go to therapy or start a new job or face any change in life, it helps to set goals. Goals are guideposts and help us succeed in new endeavors. But a goal that doesn't fit with our values is harder to commit to. For example, I might think that improving my self-confidence is a good goal because it will help me make friends at my new job. So, I pick a "confidence-boosting goal" from the internet and it tells me, "To improve your self-confidence, try taking yourself out for a solo meal of messy hot wings, and avoid worrying about what others think." My core values, and even my extended values before I honed down my list, don't include confidence, self-reliance, or independence. These are values that are important in my culture, but they hold no special meaning for me as an individual. Also, I don't eat wings and I'm trying to save money. This goal would actually go against my values of non-harm and prosperity, respectively. My dogged efforts would inevitably result in failure. The goals must be driven by—or at least compatible with—my values. Because spending time in nature is one of my values, a better goal would be: "Join a local hiking club near my new job and invite my coworkers and doggos to join us for a lunchtime nature walk."

Now it's your turn. Return to your list of values from the previous chapter. Grab a sheet of paper (or your journal) and list your values on the left side of the page. On the right side of the page jot down some of your personal goals. Draw a line between the goal and its complementary value. It's okay for the goal to be matched up with several values, but if the goal is standing there unattached, it's time for some soul-searching. Ask yourself:

- Why did I set this goal?
- Did I set this goal for myself or someone else?
- Am I still committed to this goal or am I okay letting it go?
- If I'm still committed, how can I revamp the goal to better fit my values?

Today's Act of Unconditional Self-Love

Set yourself a small, values-based goal that you can achieve today. Then go out and do it!

Today's Journaling Prompts

1. Was I surprised, scared, or intimidated by any of the goals identified above?
2. How did I feel when I achieved today's goal?

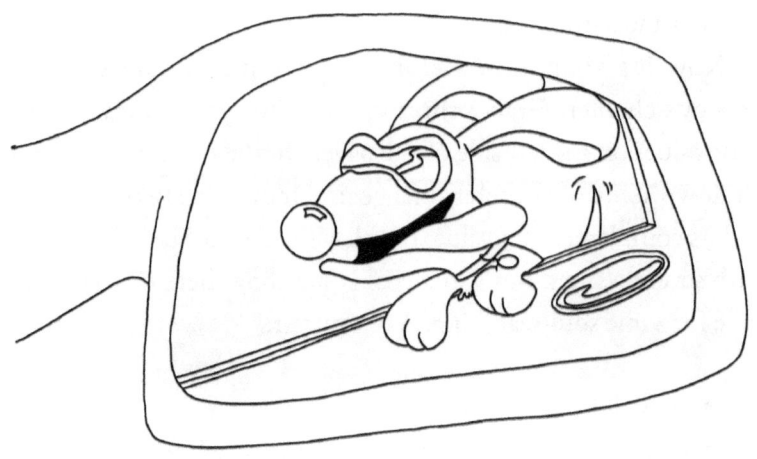

Day 16: Map Your Values to Your Life

We have been exploring values and goals in the last few chapters. You now know that goals have the greatest chance of success if they fit into your core values. If you're focusing your attention on improving relationships or enjoying a closer marriage, it wouldn't be surprising for relationships to appear in your core values. If they don't, there may be a disconnect between what you are trying to accomplish and what truly matters to you. If you say you want to quit using drugs, but sobriety or recovery don't appear in your values list, it's possible you haven't fully embraced sobriety as a core value. Perhaps you feel pressured to quit by external forces (a spouse, the court, etc.) I want to emphasize as strongly as possible that your values must support your goals in order for you to feel fulfilled and successful in life.

Now let's expand our view. Rise up to 30,000 feet and look at the big picture of your life. What do you want to accomplish in your lifetime? What experiences do you want to have? Knowing your core values gives you incredible insight into these questions.

Draw from Your Creative Side

There are many exercises that can help you develop a big picture plan. If you aren't working with a psychotherapist like myself, but you have access to a college, consider seeing a career counselor. Career counselors are great at helping people explore their values, personality traits, and interests in order to determine a career plan. I teach many of these exercises in my workshops and participants always have fun with it. These are tactile activities that you practice with all your senses—not just by talking about them. In this chapter, I'll teach you a visual/artistic version of exploring your life goals.

This time, I'd like you to find a large piece of paper—much bigger than your journal. Grab some colored pencils, markers, or fancy pens. You'll want lots of color on this page. If you have access to a large whiteboard, that's even better.

Start by choosing your centering value. This is the value that serves as a keystone for all the other values on the list. It grows out of your emotional landscape and weaves in and out of the other values. It's the one you sense most often in the highlights of your story. Common centering values include love, integrity, gratitude, spirituality, success, and my own centering value, joy. I figured out that joy was my centering value when I realized that by actively honoring the other values in my daily life, I was experiencing joy. There wasn't a separate set of activities for finding joy in my life—it was just there when I lived authentically.

Select a color that best fits your centering value. I use a bright sunny orange or dandelion yellow to represent joy. Draw a cloud in the center of your page and write your centering value inside. Make it large and loud, bold and proud.

Now draw several bubbles on the outer edges of the page. Draw one for each core value on your list.

As you fill in the outer bubbles with your other values, be playful. Use different colors, handwriting, and images to represent yourself. These are *your* inner principles! They can be fun and unique, just like you.

Next to (or inside of) each bubble, write a short sentence that captures the miracle-question version of that value. Think about what this part of your life looks like many decades from now. When a movie is made about your life, what's the Hallmark Channel version of this value? For example, family is one of my core values, so in my ideal life, I will:

- Raise a wholehearted kid who loves her authentic self
- Spend quality time (phone calls, dinners, vacations) with my parents, siblings, and friends
- Enjoy a marriage full of laughter, great sex, and stimulating conversation

This may take some time to fully articulate. Remember, Rome was not built in a day and dogs are not trained overnight. After you've mapped your values to your ideal life, I invite you to sleep on it. Spend some time chewing on the map you drew (but not literally, unlike Doggo) and then refine it. Copy it into your journal and look at it every once in a while. Is it changing as time goes on? Do any of the goals feel less authentic than they did at first drawing? Every time I complete a journal, I redraw my map in the new one. It does change slightly each time. For example, my pets were not on the first map. But I spend every waking hour with the dog and a great deal of time caring for the cats and fish. My day-to-day life has proven that my pets are part of my family, so why not include them in my map? Besides, how could I not include those heart-wrenching, hound dog eyes?

Go back and look at the values-based goals you formed after reading the last chapter. They probably look like bite-size bits of the map. The idea is that they will feel achievable and realistic as you read over them. I think you'll also feel successful and fulfilled as you accomplish your values-based goals. And your life will slowly but surely begin to look like the map you drew today. Now go take a break and eat something sweet! You deserve it.

Today's Act of Unconditional Self-Love

Make a vision board and be sure it honors your core values. Not sure what that is? Check out my website annalisasmithson.com/tools for a great video on how and why we should all be making vision boards.

Today's Journaling Prompts

1. What do I believe about values?
2. Where do these beliefs come from (family, culture, etc.)?
3. How have I honored my values today/this week/this year?

Day 17: Give Voice to Your Authentic Self

If you could leave behind all your fears and worries, all your borders and burdens, all your chains, what would be left? When you strip down to your core authentic self, who are you? In this chapter, we are going to explore your authentic self. We are going to harmonize the many words you've written in your journal, and give your authentic self a voice. You have done much of the work already. In earlier chapters you assessed your strengths, mapped your values, gave yourself permission for self-care and silence, and began to explore your emotional landscape. It's time to fit all those notes and chords together and let the final song emerge. That song is you, of course. An authentic, compassionate, loving you. If you want to feel fulfilled in your life—if you want to find meaning and truly experience self-love—I encourage you to find a way to articulate your authentic self.

The Weeks in Review

Grab your journal and flip back to some of the earlier pages we worked on together. Start with your strengths—those qualities that make you remarkable. These are the talents you can master with ease. You spend a lot of time on these talents because they give you a leg up. Whether you're a creative thinker, a master multitasker, or brilliant under pressure, these are strengths/skills/talents you enjoy using. They are part of what makes you so good at what you do. And you are doggone good!

Now move forward in your journal to the tests you took in the chapter called, "Get to Know Yourself." It's important to know where you land on the scale of introversion and extroversion. It's also fun to explore what kind of personality traits you exhibit. (Am I a debater, a mediator, a defender, or an adventurer?) By exploring your personality traits with a playful, lighthearted attitude, you can put your subconscious habits to work for you.

Now jump forward in your journal to the work you did during the chapters on self-care. I hope you have been revisiting your favorite self-care activities throughout the past weeks. Self-care is especially important at a time like this, when you're working so hard on self-exploration. Learning to love your authentic self can be tiring work. Many of us have to shed old beliefs that do not serve us, but which are deeply ingrained. We have to face the inner critic who tells us we don't deserve self-care, or compassion, or love. That critic would have us believe it's a dog-eat-dog world that we aren't good enough for. We have to end these harsh words and accept that we are good enough. We *do* deserve self-love. It is critically important to give ourselves the soothing silence of a daily meditation, the rejuvenation of a full night's sleep, the happy distraction of a good book, or the loving support of a visiting friend and their dog. Whatever self-care means for you (glance back at your journal if you don't remember), now is the time to reinstate such habits.

Move into the pages where you explored your emotional landscape (Day Five). In this chapter, you explored your feelings by logging not only how you felt, but how you knew you were feeling that way. You made connections between your heart, mind, and body.

That skill will serve you well as you learn to voice your authentic self. Your emotional landscape will alert you if you are on the right or wrong track.

Finally, look back at the work you did to explore your values. Remind yourself of your centering value—that core principle which guides your thoughts and actions. Draw a quick map of your primary values and write one sentence in each cloud, stating how you honored that value today. These values will center you when you get caught up in a barrage of "musts" and "shoulds."

What Makes You Tick?

All of these pieces fit together to help you articulate your authentic self. By the end of this chapter, you will be able to answer the question "Who are you?" in one or two sentences. Your answer will reflect all of these important components of your core self. Your answer will be unlike any other. It will be authentically you. We are going to explore some of the happiest moments in your life: the moments when you're most at ease; the biggest successes of your life; and the future goals you're most passionate about. These are your paints and you are the canvas. Let's illustrate a unique picture of you, your authentic self. Grab your journal and fill in these blanks:

I feel happiest when_____
My most successful moment was_____
My passion burns brightest for_____
I am valuable because_____
I am grateful for_____
My gut tells me_____
I have always wanted to_____
I feel most at ease when_____

I can be vulnerable about_____
I am not afraid to_____
When I have nothing else to do, I choose to_____
I love to surround myself with people who_____
When I was a kid, I always wanted to be_____
A problem I want to solve is_____
_____gets me out of bed.
I am_____
I am_____
I am_____
(Write "I am" at least ten times)

Here is an example:

- I feel happiest when I am surrounded by dogs, cats, chickens, rabbits, plants, and fish.
- My most successful moment was when I published a research article in a peer-reviewed journal.
- My passion burns brightest for ending oppression in the LGBTQ community.
- I am valuable because I offer genuine compassion for my fellow humans.
- My gut tells me to seek adventure.
- I have always wanted to swim with dolphins.
- I feel most at ease when I am in the woods.
- I am not afraid to call my senator.
- When I have nothing else to do, I choose to take on more creative projects.
- I love to surround myself with people who do most of the talking.
- When I was a kid, I always wanted to be a marine zoologist.

- A problem I want to solve is the opioid crisis.
- Helping people to grow and heal gets me out of bed extra early.
- I am a good friend, parent, and partner.
- I am a therapist.
- I am an author.
- I am a life-long learner.
- I am an animal-lover.
- I am a vegetarian.
- I am a listener.
- I am an activist.
- I am a voter.
- I am an adventurer.
- I am joyful.

Your answers to the questions above should give you some insight into what makes you tick. These are examples of moments in your life that you live authentically. Now we have to shape these insights into one or two sentences that will help you voice your authentic self. It's tough to boil all these words—values, dreams, strengths—down into one or two sentences, so be patient with yourself.

What Makes You, You?

Look at your list of answers and put on your detective cap. Search for patterns. In my answers, I see a few themes: loving animals, being a writer, and helping people. I also see that my centering value popped up again in an "I am" statement. It's okay if new answers come to mind as you're seeking patterns. The goal of this exercise is simply to gain a deeper understanding of your authentic self. Group the answers together into three categories:

1. My Gifts (the remarkable skills and strengths you enjoy using)
2. My Passions (those exciting dreams that drive you forward)
3. My Legacy (the change you wish to make in the world)

Here is an example:

1. My Gifts: healing, listening, showing compassion, writing
2. My Passions: helping people, learning, animals, adventure, nature
3. My Legacy: ending the stigma around therapy, helping the loved ones of addicts, supporting the LGBTQ community

The puzzle-pieces of values, dreams, and gifts that make you "you" should be slowly forming a clearer picture. As you articulate your authentic self, you could almost imagine that you're creating a mission statement for yourself. For example,

"I am a therapist and an author, imperfectly balanced as a mother and a partner. I use my gift of compassion and my love of animals to help people embrace the healing power of nature."

Here are a few more examples:

"I am a talented chef and I take pleasure in nourishing others, watching them enjoy my food. I want to be remembered as an artist in the kitchen."

"I am most authentic when I am traveling solo, experiencing new cultures, and trying on new languages. I embrace the freedom of a wanderer's lifestyle."

"I am a father to a large family, and nothing makes me happier than spending a weekend playing with, teaching, and loving those kids."

It may take several weeks of exploring your authentic self (both who you are and who you are not) before you are comfortable with it. Once you have given your authentic self a voice, I want you to practice sharing it with people. Your best bet is to tell a stranger. Tell lots of strangers. They will have no bias about who you have been in the past so you can fully immerse yourself in any new avenues you have discovered. It's also okay to practice with friends. The more we articulate it, the deeper and more invested we become in living authentically. Notice how it feels to share this part of yourself. Your emotions are your guideposts in moments like this, alerting you or reassuring you as needed. Listen to their direction as you mindfully explore your authentic self.

A Safe Space

A word about living authentically: People in the LGBTQ community and similarly oppressed groups may have life experiences that taught them it is safer not to express their authentic self. There may be good reason to hold back on sharing who we are until we are in a safe place. These experiences and associated feelings must be explored gently. This is when a good therapist (and a loving pet) is useful. Their absence of judgment and unconditional positive regard can enhance the healing process and help you voice your authentic self. However you choose to explore this part of yourself, just be safe. And give yourself the care you need throughout the process.

Today's Act of Unconditional Self-Love

Practice talking about the things you love about yourself. Say it out loud. Say it to your pet. Say it to your partner. Say it to a stranger.

Today's Journaling Prompts

1. What do I love about myself?
2. What makes me authentic?
3. Who am I?

Day 18: Express a "Good" Goodbye

How do you feel about saying goodbye? On a scale of gracious and heartfelt to avoiding entirely, how would you rate your ability to say goodbye?

Before you announce to the empty room, "I hate goodbyes," and cut to the next chapter, hear me out. A "good" goodbye is a positive, healthy experience. It is an opportunity for growth and will make you a richer, healthier, more compassionate person. Loving relationships deserve a moment of reminiscence and gratitude before they come to an end. Unhealthy relationships deserve a full closure with firm boundaries so the goodbye sticks. Either way, saying goodbye can be a fulfilling, positive experience for you.

If you wish to love yourself unconditionally, you must honor your boundaries and embrace your "goodbyes." People who own pets must master the art of a "good" goodbye early in the relationship, knowing that our pets have a shorter lifespan than we do. (Another lesson learned from my friend Rosie the Pug.) But also, as a human engaging in casual, professional, romantic, and even familial relationships, we must learn this challenging task on different levels.

Avoiding Goodbye

Many of us avoid goodbyes. If it was a positive relationship, such as with a therapist, a fellow student or instructor, or a colleague, we say, "See ya later," and hang on to hope that the relationship doesn't have to end. Even if chances are slim that we will continue seeing the person, we try not to actually say goodbye. We know that events like graduation and retirement often bring with them firm endings, yet we keep saying, "See ya later." If it was a negative relationship, we often disappear without closure. Legal divorces are hard to "ghost," but a bad break-up feels easier to handle if we simply say, "Call me Casper," and split.

So why do we avoid goodbyes? Some of us were taught these behaviors as children. We accept the family legacy and pass it on to our own kids without giving it much thought. Some of us are uncomfortable making other people uncomfortable. We tell white lies about why we're leaving and when we'll meet again in order to spare others' feelings. We could psychoanalyze this set of behaviors with some good, old-fashioned Jungian psychology. We could examine the symbolism of endings, the fear of death, and what "goodbye" represents in our lonesome psyches.

But why make it complicated? The simple truth is, saying goodbye hurts. It makes us feel sad. Sometimes it even makes us feel guilty. As Data (an android) says to Ishara Yar about his friend and crewmate who recently died (yes, I'm quoting *Star Trek: The Next Generation* again, season 4: episode 6, "Legacy"), "Even among humans, friendship is sometimes less an emotional response and more a familiarity.... As I experience certain sensory input patterns, my mental pathways become accustomed to them. The inputs eventually are anticipated, and even missed when absent." Even androids dislike saying goodbye. We don't like the idea of missing people who have become familiar and comfortable in our lives. So, we avoid saying goodbye to them in hopes that it will hurt less.

Embracing Goodbye

Why should I embrace saying goodbye? After all, we just agreed that it hurts, so why encourage ourselves to do it? What do words like "processing" and "closure" even mean?

Saying goodbye represents a certain loss in our lives and often leaves us with unanswered questions. We naturally want to minimize the pain—sadness, guilt, confusion—that accompanies such loss. Social psychologist Arie Kruglanski coined the phrase "need for closure" or "cognitive closure" in an attempt to explain how we deal with loss. As curious humans, we have an aversion to ambiguity. We want to make sense of any changes and loss we are experiencing by asking questions. We want answers. We want the opportunity to learn from our mistakes and sometimes create alternative endings to our relationship stories. Embracing a "good" goodbye gives us a chance to find those answers, to experience closure, and therefore move past any pain that accompanies the goodbye instead of getting lost in ambiguity.

When we acknowledge that a relationship is coming to an end, we often realize there are things we need to say out loud. We notice feelings that have gone unexpressed because we assume there's always more time. But if a loved one is nearing the end of life, we may wish to tell them how important they are to us. We may want to deliberately and intentionally voice our gratitude, respect, or love for that person. On the other hand, we may find ourselves boiling in fresh pots of anger from past hurts and that, too, needs to be processed. A "good" goodbye, even for an unhealthy relationship, can be healing.

Establishing and Respecting Boundaries

Okay, saying goodbye is important. But what does this have to do with loving my authentic self? One word: boundaries.

Healthy boundaries are the core ingredient of self-love and all love. Love without boundaries is like a beach without sand. Rocky shores exist but they're painful to your bare feet. When you learn how to say goodbye to the right relationship at the right time, you offer yourself the love and compassion you need in that moment. You honor your human need for closure.

Therapy provides an opportunity to be honest with ourselves about how much saying goodbye can hurt. It also shows us how it feels to get real closure. As my clients and I are nearing the end of our journey together, I always invite them to think about how we might say goodbye to each other during our final session. I give them many weeks to think about this, as it could be the first time they are ever attempting a deliberate, intentional, "good" goodbye. Benji's participation in this stage of therapy is poignant and painful. Clients often tell themselves they can call me if they need me. But Benji only chews on phones instead of talking on them so his goodbye looks like any other end-of-session snuggle. That's why it's important to cry in the moment, laugh when inspired, and embrace our feelings fully. We talk about the "good" goodbye, practice saying it, and finally, we end the therapy journey together. Likewise, you and I are ending this journey together. As a reader and a writer, we have formed a certain bond. Now the relationship is coming to an end and we have to say goodbye. But just like you, and just like most other humans, I don't like goodbyes. So, let's stick together for a few more days. I want to talk to you about your next steps.

Today's Act of Unconditional Self-Love

Rid yourself of something that no longer serves you: clean out a kitchen drawer or a closet, or even a whole room, or just the trash bag in your car. This is a simple but powerful symbol of a good goodbye.

Today's Journaling Prompts

1. Whom have I had to say goodbye to when I wasn't ready?
2. Whom do I want to say goodbye to, whether they're ready or not?
3. What part of myself am I ready to say goodbye to?

Day 19: Love Yourself in a Post-Pandemic World

The year 2020 was a dangerous roller coaster ride (just not the fun kind), whipping its riders back and forth at a nauseating velocity. With the rise of coronavirus, a sharp economic downturn, and growing unrest, nobody can claim to be unaffected by that year. The normalcy we enjoyed in the pre-pandemic world has been shaken and, for many, this has led to traumatic events that have upended lives.

Psychological trauma is created as a response to a crisis or series of crises. Common examples are natural disasters, accidents, and assaults. At the heart of any trauma-inducing incident is the sense of your safety and security being compromised. Throughout covid, countless people have had their feelings of safety and security shattered from losing loved ones, losing jobs, and having their way of life disturbed in unprecedented ways. We all know people that have felt the hardships of this pandemic. These times have created fear, anxiety, sickness, and for more than a million people worldwide, death. Living through the time of coronavirus fits the very definition of a traumatic experience.

Even as we cope with this trauma on an individual level, it is also taking its toll on our society as a whole. Jena M. Ostrowski, a licensed clinical social worker and trained first responder, explains,

"We are in the midst of experiencing a chronic collective trauma and we don't know when it's going to be over. We're coping with hundreds of thousands of deaths related to covid and even people who escape the illness itself could experience psychological harm. Think about how society-wide traumas of the past have impacted entire generations: the holocaust, slavery, 9/11... the impact of those traumatic events are still with us. That kind of long-term psychological distress to a large group of people is what we call a 'collective chronic trauma." So as the pandemic carries on, how can we as individuals and as a society begin to work through all these feelings of insecurity, uncertainty, disruption, and grief? Essentially, how can we still foster our self-love?

Signs of Psychological Trauma

First we must acknowledge the signs of trauma and what effect it is having on our lives. We can respond emotionally with feelings like anger, guilt, or shame or cognitively with mood swings, confusion, and nightmares. Sometimes behavioral signs include hypervigilance, avoidance, or isolation (we had no choice but to endure isolation during quarantine). Physical signs could be aches and pains, edginess, or insomnia. Lastly, our psychological state could be affected with anxiety, depression, or panic attacks. Regardless of how trauma shows itself, it drastically affects our ability to maintain self-care and self-love. Take Perry as an example.

Perry recently called me with complaints of anxiety. They reported excessive worry that was difficult to control and noticed their relationships suffering. I asked when they started feeling this way and the onset of their anxiety coincided with the start of quarantine. As the months passed, Perry had created a habit of staying up all night scrolling through news feeds digging for information on covid-19 and its political fall-out. Throughout the day they become quick tempered and argumentative. The further we dug into the anxiety, the more signs pointed to Perry suffering a psychological trauma from the experience. Their signs of trauma were hyper-vigilance, insomnia, edginess, anger, headaches, and more. Perry was one of many clients who called me with similar complaints in 2020 and 2021. They were not alone. Millions of people experienced (and expressed) this trauma uniquely.

After acknowledging the trauma and the ways it manifests in our day to day lives, how can we as individuals begin to heal? What's more, how can we begin to heal as a collective?

The road to self-love and self-care from here is a bit murky. As Ostrowski continues, "We don't know what the rehabilitative process will look like for our generation or the next. Self-care is good, but it's not enough. Therapy and medication will also help, of course. I think the key to resilience is support. It's important to create a cohort of people you can lean on, what they're calling 'quarantine pods'. We have to truly connect with the people around us, given that we have to socialize so carefully now. To be able laugh with the people we love, to feel safe again, that's how we heal. Furthermore, we have to be gentle with ourselves."

With the social distancing, stay-at-home orders, and shuttering of recreational businesses we all experienced isolation. A trauma-induced mindset can fester when we are all alone. Even as we emerge from this isolation, we can continue to experience lingering side-effects. As Ostrowski points out, it is imperative for us to stay connected with our loved ones and confidants. By maintaining these connections, we are reestablishing our sense of security in ourselves and with the people around us.

Loving Yourself Through Trauma

With a collective trauma unfolding before us, the ability to practice self-love is becoming strained. From personal safety to livelihood, many of us have entered 'survival mode'. We sacrifice a lot of the energy we previously used for self-care activities to keep ourselves afloat. In many cases we try to downplay the psychological impact of what happened in the pandemic. For some it's as simple as being unable to go to the gym while others had their time absorbed with supporting kids in virtual schooling. No matter how big or small, we all made changes and took losses to our self-love habits. What has changed in your life since covid-19 swept across the world? How has this changed the way you care for yourself? The way you show yourself love and grace?

Instead of beating yourself up over these losses, give yourself some compassion. You have undoubtedly had to offer kind words to others who are struggling. Allow yourself to say these words to yourself and to acknowledge that you are a part of the collective. As covid-19 continues to change the world, focus on changing your personal expectations. Many of our boundaries and goals have shifted and we can't expect the same things for ourselves as we did in the pre-pandemic world.

Human connection builds resilience. Being open, communicative, and genuine with the people around you will help to ease the impact of trauma. Return to the 'love list' you wrote in the beginning of your journal and ask yourself, when was the last time you genuinely connected with these people? Is there anyone you haven't heard from in awhile? If so, try reaching out and making that genuine connection. Consider writing an old-fashioned letter using pen and paper. The act of writing is healing and for many people, the experience of receiving a hand-written letter is surprising and joyful.

Today's Act of Unconditional Self-Love

Healing often occurs through helping. Many in these times can use a helping hand so extend yours to the community. Consider donating food to a local soup kitchen or volunteer for a crisis hotline. This will not only help in your healing process, boosting your feelings of connectedness, self-worth, gratitude and compassion, it will also help build a sense of security in others.

Today's Journaling Prompts

1. What has changed in my life since covid-19 swept across our country?
2. How has this changed the way I care for myself? The way I show myself love and grace?

Day 20: Know When You Need a Tune-Up

For the past 20 days you and I have been on a journey together. You've thoughtfully paced this book and filled the pages of your journal, embracing the opportunity to tell your story. You've been kind enough to witness my own story through these pages. We've assessed your strengths, explored your values, and given your authentic self a voice. We have externalized the vicious belief that you are somehow the problem. We have explored the gentle solution of filling that empty space with pure, unconditional self-compassion. I hope you've developed a kind-but-firm mindfulness habit and a healthy obsession with self-care. My sincerest hope is that you've tossed this book to the side on many occasions so you could simply bask in your pet's unconditional love.

You deserve unconditional love.

And with the enormous amount of effort you've put into this journey, you are beginning to feel the spark of self-love warming your heart. But unconditional love is a life-long journey and so far, we've only given it twenty days. As you may recall from the introduction, twenty days isn't enough to crystallize a new habit in your neural pathways. You need at least twenty-one days to develop a new habit (you're nearly there!) and even then, you don't stop working on it. So, what's next?

Your Aftercare Plan

If you were a client in my therapy practice and we were closing out our twentieth and final session, I would come to you with a plan. Really, an actual document called the "Aftercare Plan." But in addition to that—I would come to you with more than a faded Xerox to fill in the blanks—I would bring you my compassion, my tears, and my heartfelt gratitude. The therapeutic relationship is just as important to us, the clinicians, as it is to you, the client.

Imagine that you and I are on a road trip together. We've got the windows down and visors popped. The radio is tuned to our favorite music and there's a map spread across my lap. You're in the driver's seat, of course, and Benji is in the back, secretly taste-testing our snacks. I'm here to help you plan the route and offer navigation tips when you need me. But you're the one in control of the wheel. You get to choose when to accelerate and how fast we'll go. You also have access to the brake and can slow us down any time. You can even stop the car if you wish. You're the master of this journey and I am your respectful navigator. Until, of course, we reach your destination. Then it's time for me to hand over the well-loved map, marked with all the side-trips and shortcuts and leisurely round-abouts we discovered together. At that point, the road trip is over, and you've got all the skills you need to ride solo. But how could two people (and a dog) not experience a powerful bond after such a journey? I want my clients to know that my laughter and my tears, while elicited in empathy, were just as powerful for me as they were for you. So, when it's time to draft an aftercare plan (or pass along the map, to stick with our metaphor) it's a poignant moment for me, too.

The next steps after therapy are to tape your aftercare plan to the mirror and follow it faithfully. It lists all the components of your wellness toolbox (the things you learned in therapy like thought-stopping, grounding, emotion regulation, etc.). It also has a daily maintenance plan that includes self-care, a list of potential triggers for a recurrence of the problem, and an action plan for those triggers. And it has my phone number, of course. Because a healthy lifestyle, like a dependable car, needs the occasional tune-up.

The next steps after reading this book are a little different. Your journal has all the components of an aftercare plan and you can continue using it. I *encourage* you to keep using it—journal with wild abandon about your life and dreams! Journal creatively and absurdly. Be weird in your journal. Write, draw, paste, and paint your way through every adorable journal on your shelf. I promise that once you create the habit, journaling will blossom into a healing experience for you.

But there must be more to your next steps than a journal and an aftercare plan. Your feelings of self-love are still tender. It's a new and vulnerable experience. For self-love to become unconditional, it must be nurtured. Your next step is to find someone like Benji or Rosie. Find a therapist like me or Marcy. Welcome a therapeutic relationship into your life. Turn this self-help jaunt into a full-on road trip with a map, a navigator, and your very own therapy dog in the backseat. I wish I could shout these words from the rooftops and paste them across billboards: There is no shame in asking for help! If you don't have access to a professional therapist, seek help in other ways. Go to a pastor, call an old teacher, join a mentorship program, or find a coach. Call your friends. Call your mom. Call anyone, just so long as you don't do this alone. Your next step, dear reader, is to lean on someone else.

Today's Act of Unconditional Self-Love

Go back to your list of self-care ideas and commit to doing one today.

Today's Journaling Prompts

1. What do I love about myself?
2. What do I want to change about myself?
3. What is my next step?

Day 21: Reward Yourself

Congratulations! You stuck with this journey to the end. After all this work, I hope you're ready to reward yourself. Perhaps, like many of us, you still struggle with rewarding yourself. I want to share with you one last story about Benji.

Benji and I were recently invited to visit a Girl Scout Troop to help them earn their animal-helper badges. Remembering how tough it was to be a twelve-year-old girl, I wanted to pass on this message of unconditional love to them. I wanted to help them understand that it is not necessary to meet any conditions in order to be loved. We don't have to weigh a certain amount, achieve a certain grade, or hide our true selves to deserve love. All humans— and doggos—deserve unconditional love. Furthermore, love should be both internal and external. We deserve love from others as well as from ourselves. And whether we "succeed" or not, we must still practice self-care and learn to reward ourselves for hard work. That's where things got fuzzy.

"Why would you reward yourself if you don't succeed?"

"Like, why reward yourself for a bad grade?"

"Does 'reward' really mean 'dessert'? I'm too 'fat' already."

"Is a reward the same as an award?"

"How do you reward yourself?"

All excellent questions—except perhaps that bit about being 'fat.' That one was just hurtful. So how, exactly, do you reward yourself? Enter Benji, stage left. No one teaches the art of the reward like Benjamin Sisko Franklin. Benji loves a good reward. I asked for two helpers, and we had no shortage of volunteers. Two enthusiastic scouts received a treat bag, a box of Benji's favorite toys, and a set of instructions on how to train a dog. It was the same kind of instructions you received on Day Six: "Tackling Self Doubt." Thus began a hilarious fifteen minutes of trying to teach Benji to roll over. It's hard enough to teach a dog a new trick when you're not the handler. But Benji has his own quirks of sneaking into the toy box whenever it's down at eye-level. He doesn't always wait for success to help himself to a reward.

Benji is quick to sit whenever he's asked. Even though he is fully trained to sit down without a treat, the girls still gave him one each time he complied. He's less willing to lay down with a verbal command. I let the girls figure out on their own that he needs a hand signal for that command. Eventually they convinced him to lay down and gave him another reward. At that point he needed a break. Everyone paused for a quick stretch and let Benji chase a ball for a few minutes. Then back to work. We were on to the hard part. How to get a dog to roll over? Do you lay down on the floor and demonstrate rolling to him? All that gets you is a face full of puppy kisses, as the scouts discovered. Do you push him over and roll his body for him? That might work, but is it really okay to force a dog's body to move? No, it is not. Do you take a toy and swirl it around in a "roll over" motion? Actually, that worked! Benji completed the feat on his own and the room erupted in cheers, applause, and laughter. Benji's ultimate reward was a chorus of "Good boy," and belly rubs.

Happily, the girls were so focused on the activity that they forgot about their earlier confusion. (Mindfulness in action!) So, I broke it down for them. The art of the reward for a good boy like Benji doesn't require total success from the start. In fact, mini rewards throughout the learning process helped him learn faster. And no, the rewards didn't have to be food, although Benji never minds extra snacks. Treats, toys, praise, and belly rubs all motivated him to keep working hard. When he needed a break (or what we call self-care) he told me with his body language. A quick break chasing his ball was all the self-care he needed before getting back to work. And when he finally achieved his goal, the support of his new friends was the best reward he could ask for. Now, if Benji hadn't learned to roll over during that session, would he still deserve some belly rubs for all that hard work? Of course! The same goes for us humans. We'll never be perfect, and we'll rarely nail it (whatever "it" is) on the first try. Even so, we deserve to be loved, we need self-care, and it's okay to reward ourselves.

Honoring Yourself Unconditionally

So now it's your turn. You've been working hard for the past month. You took on the challenge of separating your lovely self from the problems that plagued you. You've learned to meditate and incorporate mindfulness into your life. You assessed your strengths and personality, created a highly personalized self-care plan, and tackled any self-doubts. You explored your ideal life and your emotional landscape, then named the values that will lead you to such a life. You learned to say goodbye to what no longer serves you. I hope you have come to believe that you deserve unconditional love, regardless of what problems you face or mistakes you've made. And now you deserve a reward. But what, exactly, is a reward?

A reward is every bit as personal as a self-care activity. It simply depends on what brings you pleasure. It can be anything that makes you feel happy, fulfilled, grateful, or relaxed. A reward can be food or fun, it can be quick or leisurely, it can be literally anything. I only ask that whatever you choose for your reward, it makes you feel loved. After all, you deserve to feel loved. *You* are amazing.

Today's Act of Unconditional Self-Love

Reward yourself!

Today's Journaling Prompts

1. What's different about me now from when I started this journey?
2. What am I thinking, feeling, and deciding in this moment?
3. What am I going to do next, in the near future?

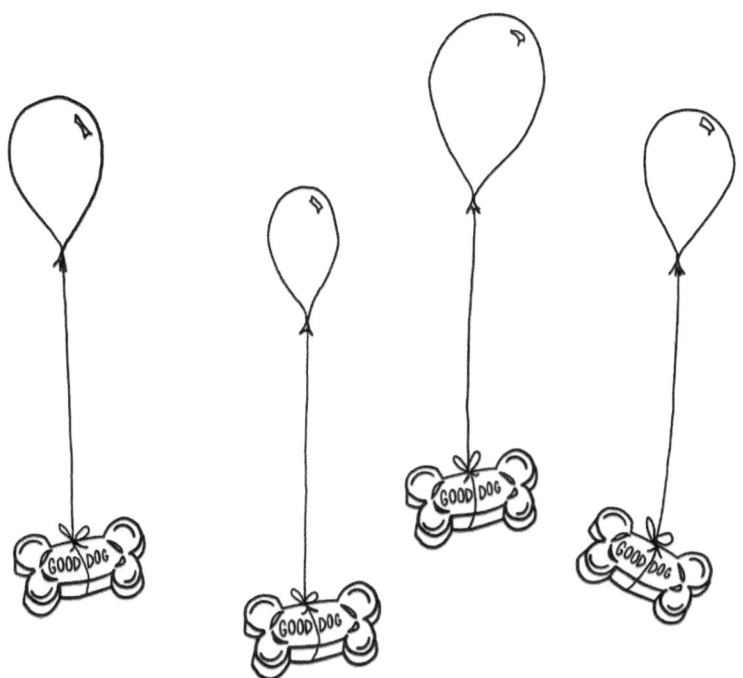

Conclusion

What have the past 21 days been like for you? How does it feel to start exploring those tender emotions related to self-love? I hope self-compassion, self-forgiveness, and self-respect are all closer to the forefront of your thoughts, feelings, and actions. I hope you now have a robust toolbox full of practices to maintain your mental health and wellness. My dearest wish is that you are able to show yourself the kind of wholesome, unconditional love that your dog shows you.

If you are still struggling to solidify your habit of self-love, that's okay. Remember that there's nothing magical about 21 days. Your brain is forming a new neural pathway to establish this new habit, yes, but it's only a foundation. The next 21 days will strengthen and reaffirm this new habit. And the 21 days following that will bring even more ease and grace to your habit of self-love. But it's an ongoing journey, and you're still at the very beginning. Be kind to yourself.

Everyone's childhood, former relationship with self-love, and past experiences with therapy are different. Because of these differences, the habit of self-love will come easier for some and harder for others. We, as humans, are unique individuals with varying needs and abilities. Although habit-experts most often say that 21 days are all you need, some psychologists say it may take 66 days or even 90 days to get your brain fully on board with a new habit. Self-love is worth the effort, so here's what I suggest—

Don't stop now.

Keep practicing these habits.

Continue loving yourself unconditionally.

Look through your journal and think about what it was like to do each activity throughout the past 21 days. Which one stands out to you the most? Which one brought you the most joy or the most discomfort and therefore the biggest change? Let's return to that activity and fully embrace it. Let's spend another 21 days together practicing just that one activity.

There's no right or wrong answer here, everyone has a different practice that stands out for them. For example, you could spend the next 21 days:

- Practicing a daily meditation devoted to Loving-Kindness.
- Writing a gratitude list at the end of each day.
- Committing to a physical self-care routine, like daily stretching.

I recommend thumbing through this book once more to look for inspiration as you set your next 21-day goal. Here are a few more ideas to kickstart PHASE TWO of your self-love habit:

- Return to your list of best qualities from days 6 and 10. Expand the list so there are 21 qualities. Every day for the next 21 days dive deep into one of your positive qualities. What do you love about that strength? How did you come by it? How does it make you a better person? How does it fit into your feelings of self-love, self-compassion, and self-respect?

- Return to day 2, exploring the love of your inner circle (your love list). Expand the list so there are 21 names and each day for the next 21 days write about why you love that person and how they make you feel loved. Consider sending that person a text, email, or old-fashioned thank you card for being who they are.
- Return to the section of day 6 on challenging negative thought patterns. Spend the next 21 days creating a thought log, writing down each of the negative thoughts you experience that day. Then write a positive reframe for the new thought you're going to replace it with.
- Return to days 11 to 13 and create a 21-day self-care activity plan. Keep the activities small and simple, like taking three deep breaths before you enjoy the first sip of delicious coffee in the morning. Commit to it for the entire three weeks and notice how your self-care activities boost your feelings of self-love.

Whatever direction you choose for your next level of self-love, you're off to a wonderful start. You've already built the foundation you need to banish negative thoughts and free yourself from stress, overwhelm, depression, and anxiety. Now, for your final journaling prompt: **How and why will I continue practicing unconditional self-love?**

Thank you so much for the honor of joining you on your self-love journey.

Happiness: ecstatic, joyful, excited, sensuous, energetic, cheerful, creative, hopeful, peaceful, content, thoughtful, intimate, loving, trusting, nurturing, daring, fascinating, stimulating, amused, playful, relaxed, serene, secure, grateful, thankful

Sadness: depressed, grieved, lonely, bored, tired, guilty, ashamed, remorseful, stupid, inferior, isolated, apathetic, empty

Anger: enraged, annoyed, critical, judged, hateful, selfish, mad, hostile, hurt, distant, sarcastic, frustrated, jealous, irritated, skeptical, bitter

Fear: terrified, apprehensive, anxious, insecure, helpless, rejected, confused, bewildered, discouraged, insignificant, inadequate, embarrassed, overwhelmed

Disgust: loathing, disapproving, disappointed, awful, judged, revolted, repugnant

Surprise: startled, confused, amazed, excited, shocked, dismayed, disillusioned, perplexed, astonished, awed

Download worksheets at www.annalisasmithson.com/tools.

Abundance
Accomplishment
Accountability
Accuracy
Achievement
Acknowledgment
Action
Adventure
Ambition
Authenticity
Awareness
Balance
Beauty
Calm
Cheerfulness
Clarity
Collaboration
Comfort
Community
Compassion
Competition
Confidence
Connectedness

Contentment
Contribution
Control
Cooperation
Courage
Creativity
Curiosity
Discipline
Discovery
Ease
Empathy
Empowerment
Energy
Enthusiasm
Environment
Excellence
Fairness
Faith
Fame
Family
Flexibility
Focus
Freedom
Friendship
Fulfillment
Fun
Generosity
Gentleness
Gratitude
Growth
Happiness

Harmony
Health
Helpfulness
Honesty
Honor
Humility
Humor
Independence
Inspiration
Integrity
Intelligence
Intimacy
Joy
Kindness
Knowledge
Learning
Liveliness
Love
Loyalty
Nature
Open-mindedness
Participation
Partnership
Passion
Patience
Peace
Perfection
Persistence
Philanthropy
Power
Productivity

Prosperity
Recognition
Respect
Romance
Security
Self-esteem
Service
Significance
Simplicity
Sobriety
Spirituality
Spontaneity
Stability
Status
Strength
Success
Teamwork
Tolerance
Tradition
Trust
Understanding
Unity
Vitality
Wealth
Wisdom

Download worksheets at www.annalisasmithson.com/tools.

TIPS FOR ACTIVE LISTENING

Active listening is the art of mindfulness in conversation. It is listening with your whole body, mind, and heart. Once you've trained your body to give the cues of listening, and learned to quiet the mind of internal chatter, your heart can really hear the person's story. And there is no greater gift than being asked to witness another person's story. Here are some tips for active listening:

Body

- Face the speaker
- Uncross your arms
- Make eye contact
- Hold your tongue except for encouragers ("Oh," "Uh-huh," "And?")
- Nod when you understand
- Let your face express your feelings (confusion, surprise, etc.)
- Save questions for later (they will probably answer them if you let them keep speaking)

Mind

- Avoid making judgments
- Avoid jumping to conclusions

- Paraphrase in your mind to stay focused on their words
- Think about what they're saying (not what you're planning to say)
- Avoid offering solutions (that would be problem-solving rather than active listening)
- Stay focused

Heart

- Feel your compassion
- Embrace your empathy
- Exercise patience
- Be comfortable with small silences

At the end of a heavy bout of active listening you will be tired. You have used mental, emotional, and even physical energy to stay present and focused on the speaker's story. You should be able to paraphrase their key points when they are finished speaking. You may have clarifying questions or wish to reflect what's in your heart. This is also an important part of active listening. Just be sure to give them some space (a small silence) before you begin responding. They may actually need more time to continue speaking. And you may need a mental rest.

Download worksheets at www.annalisasmithson.com/tools.

SUGGESTED READING LIST

Brown, Brene (2013). *Daring greatly: How the courage to be vulnerable transforms the way we live, love, parent and lead.* London: Portfolio Penguin.

Brown, Stuart & Vaughan, Christopher (2009). *Play: how it shapes the brain, opens the imagination, and invigorates the soul.* New York: Avery.

Hari, Johann (2018). *Lost connections: Uncovering the real causes of depression-- and the unexpected solutions.* New York: Bloomsbury.

Kabat-Zin, Jon (2018). *Falling Awake: How to Practice Mindfulness in Everyday Life* 1st Edition. New York: Hatchette Book Group, Inc.

Korb, Alex (2015). *The upward spiral: using neuroscience to reverse the course of depression, one small change at a time.* Oakland, CA. New Harbinger Publications.

Sincero, Jen (2013). *You are a badass: How to stop doubting your greatness and start living an awesome life.* Philadelphia: Running Press.

Schuster, Tara (2020). *Buy yourself the f*cking lilies: and other rituals to fix your life, from someone who's been there.* New York: The Dial Press.

Singer, Michael (2007). *The untethered soul: The journey beyond yourself.* Oakland, CA: New Harbinger Publications.

Tolle, Eckhart (2005). *A new earth: awakening to your life's purpose.* Toronto: Penguin.

Winfrey, Oprah. (2017). *The Wisdom of Sundays: Life changing insights from super soul conversations* (audiobook) New York: Flatiron Books.

1. ˆ *"Gallup 2019 Global Emotions Report," Gallup, 2019*
2. ˆ *"Major Depression," National Institute of Mental Health, 2019*
3. ˆ *"Understand the Facts," Anxiety and Depression Association of America, n.d.*
4. ˆ *Is it really necessary to have a dog of your own to appreciate this analogy? Not at all! If you've ever bonded with a dog, cat, or other animal that made you feel warm and fuzzy, you've experienced this kind of connection. You've been loved unconditionally by a critter that doesn't judge the way humans sometimes do.*
5. ˆ *Ivan Pavlov is the famous scientist who discovered the concept of classical conditioning. His studies demonstrated that dogs would salivate automatically when shown food and proved they could be conditioned to salivate in other circumstances by associating the food to a new stimulus, such as a bell ringing. This influenced psychologists to develop the school of behaviorism, which states that with the right conditioning humans are capable of making significant changes in our thoughts, feelings, and habits.*
6. ˆ *Lally, P., van Jaarsveld, C. H. M., Potts, H. W. W., & Wardle, J. (2009). How are habits formed: Modelling habit formation*

in the real world. European Journal of Social Psychology, 40(6), 998–1009. doi:10.1002/ejsp.674

7. ^ *Prochaska, James O.; DiClemente, Carlo C. (2005). "The transtheoretical approach". In Norcross, John C.; Goldfried, Marvin R. (eds.). Handbook of psychotherapy integration. Oxford series in clinical psychology (2nd ed.). Oxford; New York: Oxford University Press. pp. 147–171.*

8. ^ *de Shazer S., Dolan Y., Korman H., Trepper T., McCollum E., Berg I.K. More Than Miracles: State of the Art of Solution-Focused Brief Therapy. Oxon, UK: Routledge; 2012.*

9. ^ *If you struggle to identify your feelings, go to the Worksheets section of this book and explore the emotion chart.*

10. ^ *Boccia, M., Piccardi, L., & Guariglia, P. (2015). The Meditative Mind: A Comprehensive Meta-Analysis of MRI Studies. BioMed research international, 2015, 419808. https://doi.org/10.1155/2015/419808*

11. ^ *Laska, K. M., Gurman, A. S., Wampold, B. E. (2014). Expanding the lens of evidence-based practice in psychotherapy: A common factors perspective. Psychotherapy, 51, 467-481.*

12. ^ *If you are struggling with housing or food, there is help available. Call the national housing line at 800-569-4287 and ask for a local agency. The local agency can direct you to additional resources near you.*

13. ^ *The debate continues among my friends and colleagues. Some insist that television is a vital part of our personal and cultural identity. The greatest visual and performing arts of the 20th century were achieved on the silver screen and the 21st century is being hailed as the golden age of television. People bond over thought-provoking programs and grow through heart-rending stories that transcend entertainment. Others point out that if meaningful self-care could be achieved with television, we would*

have five generations of enlightened, self-compassionate people. These folks believe that the risk for brainless binge-watching makes TV a dangerous habit. What's your opinion? Does watching television count as self-care for you? How do you feel after a few hours with your favorite show?

After ten years of studying anthropology and wandering around the world in a lonely career path, Annalisa Smithson, LPC (aka Lylly) decided to make a change. She returned to Pennsylvania, earned a master's in counseling from Lehigh University, and met the dog of her dreams. Together, she and Benji opened Unleashed Counseling, an animal-assisted therapy practice for folks overcoming depression, anxiety, and addiction. The rest is history. Now she spends her free time outside doing yoga with her kiddo, backpacking with her gorgeous spouse, and floating around on paddleboards. Connect with her at www.annalisasmithson.com or @UnleashedCounseling.

ABOUT THE ARTIST

Cory Derer has the creative bookworm's dream-job: she is an assistant librarian by day and a cartoonist by night. Her wild imagination and clever eye brings beauty to the world through multiple mediums including photography, jewelry, pottery, and paint. Cory works to incorporate her love of nature and sunny sense of humor into each piece of art she creates. She studied at the Moore College of Art and Design before abandoning traditional academia to open her own portrait studio, C. Wilson Photography, Inc. She now lives in the Philadelphia suburbs with her husband, four children, and two adorable dogs. Connect with her on Facebook @CoryWilsonDerer.

Emotional Support Animals: Clinician's Guide to ESA Assessments and Recommendation Letters (2021). Magic happens when a client successfully incorporates an emotional support animal (ESA) into their mental health treatment. The unconditional love of a bonded animal is a wonderful, healing experience. But *when* is it appropriate to write an ESA recommendation letter for your client? And *how* do you complete the assessment? This guide fills a critical gap for counselors, therapists, and social workers. Learn how to educate your clients on the purpose of an ESA, explore the ethical implications of doing ESA assessments, and discover the five key questions that need to be answered before writing an ESA letter.

Self Care Journal: Notes from the Desk of Doggo (2022). This "not-so-guided journal" is for stressed-out folks who happen to love dogs and want to create more self-love. Fill the pages with your thoughts, feelings, quotes, art, affirmations, and anything else that inspires you. If you're struggling to find inspiration, look no further than the adjoining page. There, you'll find a letter from Benji, the therapy dog, that includes a trusty self-care tip — it may be just what you need to get your creativity flowing.

ACKNOWLEDGMENTS

I owe a world of gratitude to my village for making this book happen. Thank you, first and foremost, to my clients, whose compassion and courage are changing the world. And of course, to John and River, for your patience and loving support during this roller coaster ride. You are my heart. I also wish to thank Cory, who brought my ideas to life with her playful art.

I naively believed there were just two steps to becoming an author: first you write it, then you publish it. I'm so grateful for the team of professionals who educated me and helped me navigate the dozens of steps in between: to my writing coach, Rachel, whose 5am wakeup calls got me through the first draft and across the finish line; to Pete and Marisa, my talented editors, who polished my rocky manuscript into a gem of a book; to my brilliant beta readers, Jena, Mark, and Molly, who boosted my sense of humor and sense of order within these pages, and to my team at Unleashed Counseling: Maggie, Nicole, Leah, Heather, Cleo, and Sandy, who make work feel like play.

Thank you to my parents for instilling in me a love of books, my siblings for teaching me to dodge apple cores, my best friend Danielle for always cheering me on, and my nieces for giving me the gift of time to actually write.

Although they are anonymous, I'd be remiss if I didn't acknowledge my recovery partner and home group; without sobriety I never would have found the courage to share my work. Thank you, family.

And finally, I will forever be grateful to Benjamin Sisko Franklin, the doggo who inspired this book and reminds me every day to love myself unconditionally.